Baby of

A Birthmother's Journey Through Adoption

By Laura Anderson

To the young girl who lost her sunshine, keep going, it gets better.

Acknowledgements

There are so many people I could thank for getting me to where I am today. Please know that even if you are not specifically mentioned below, if I know you then you have been a part of my journey in some form or another. So, thank you.

To my Mum and my Sister

Thank you for being two of the strongest women that I know. Thank you for being by my side through everything and for being fanastic role models as women, mothers and as friends. I can never explain how much you both mean to me. I will love you forever.

To Peggy

Thank you for helping me to be the best version of myself. Thank you for encouraging me and aiding me to write this book. Thank you for being my personal cheerleader. Mostly, thank you for being such a good friend.

"There is no greater agony than bearing an untold story inside you."

Maya Angelou.

This book is dedicated to every birthparent with an untold story inside them. May this book ensure you know that you're not alone, and may it inspire you to share your own story, once you feel able to.

xx

PROLOGUE

It was up to the Panel now. I had done everything I possibly could to prove that I could be a good mother, and that I should be able to take my baby home. I'd had my evaluations, I had met with my social worker every time she asked, shown her around our home and I'd been open and honest about where I was in my life mentally. We had volunteered our life story to Social Services and answered any and all questions they had. We had gone above and beyond, but they had been erratic and inefficient and run out of time. All that could be done now was to sit and wait for a team of people, who had never met me, to decide if their interpretation of all the information they had, if all the words on the paper in front of them, were enough to release my baby from the hospital and into my arms.

As I sat in the Neonatal Intensive Care Unit, alive to every breathe my little one took, I listened to the other babies crying. I heard the all too familiar sound of machines alerting in the other rooms, and the doctors and nurses chatting, never quite out of ear shot, so you always knew everyone else's business, which of course meant they knew mine too. I sat waiting for the ringing of the phone amongst the jungle of sounds. Many times, it rang, and every time it was not the call I was waiting for. Until finally, it was.

My mind flashed back to the start of all of this, when I thought having a baby, a wonderful partner and living happily ever after was easy. I remember how, once upon a time, I was just a normal, albeit incredibly young, mum. This situation now,

1

in fact my entire life, was a world away from the happy go lucky girl who once wrongly assumed that life could be a fairytale. In truth, my adult life started out more like a dark tragedy. A nightmare.

I took a deep breathe in and watched as the nurse put the phone down and walked towards the room where I sat watching over my baby. In that moment, the world fell away, and my heart sank. I told myself the worst before a word even left that nurse's mouth. This was it, the moment I would find out if my baby would finally come home with me.

Chapter One
Prince Charming

Being bullied at school was the catalyst for a lot of things that started to come out in my personality in my teenage years. Having virtually no positive recognition from my peers made me yearn to be liked and accepted and yet I found that hard to come by. I became someone who liked to be alone, despite craving acceptance, the two didn't seem to mesh well and, unfortunately, I developed some bad habits that proved hard to shake. Being the victim of bullying for years, even though I was told that if I ignored them they would go away, created a need in me for favourable attention. I wanted those who hurt me to like me. I wanted a day, or maybe just an hour, when I didn't feel less than everyone else. I wanted to matter to people, to really matter. The way you do when you're sick, or you're going through something hard, and people feel sorry for you. People can't hate someone who is ill or sad, that would be wrong.

One night I reached for the nail scissors, and I scratched myself on the arms. I didn't want to hurt myself, only for it to look that way so people would pay attention to me. Mostly, the scratches just turned red and bumpy, except for one where I pressed harder than intended and blood bubbled to the surface. The burning pain made me regret it instantly. In the morning, the scratches were still visible and during one class I purposefully let my sleeve ride up, revealing them to the girl sitting next to me. She saw, and so did the teacher, Mr Robinson, which was not part of the plan. He asked me to stay after class, and my classmate hung back too. Both were clearly concerned, and they demanded to know what had happened. I was caught in the spotlight and spoke without thinking. I told them I was self-harming in response to being abused. It was a complete fabrication but the instant I said it I couldn't take it back. Looking back, I wonder whether this was the moment when my life turned.

I don't even know where the words came from, but I panicked and was too scared to crawl out of the very deep hole I'd fallen into. When Mr Robinson said that he intended to speak to my parents, I almost fell to my knees begging him not to. I pleaded that I would do anything he asked if he didn't tell them. Shockingly, and in hindsight quite worryingly, he agreed and said that if I saw the school nurse then he wouldn't say a word. I couldn't agree fast enough and the following day I kept my promise and went to see her. She made me promise not to do it again and sent me on my way.

One of the worst things about high school is that everyone knows everybody's business. My 'self-harming', and the stupid excuse I made up for it, had spread around the school like wildfire, and was totally out of my control. People kept asking me what happened and checking on me, asking if I was okay. This was exactly what I had wanted, which is the worst thing that could have happened. In my vulnerable state of mind, I learned that lying earned me the kind of attention I craved, and that was such a bad way of thinking about this situation. I went from wishing I could take it back, to lapping up the sympathy, even though I recognised it was mostly feigned by people who just wanted to chat to the 'person of the moment'.

The next week, I was old news, and nobody cared anymore. But the horrible notion that lies got attention stuck, and I couldn't shake it off even when I tried. I went to the doctor to confess I needed help with this but instead of owning my mistakes, I doubled down. I was given a form to complete to score my mood and immaturely ticked almost every box. While some were accurate, most I ticked simply because it would lead to being asked more questions, being invited to talk and being heard. I was sent to therapy and asked about episodes of depression, my eating habits and trauma, tick, tick, tick. It was like having my own very special someone who existed just to give me everything I needed, and it was like a drug. To get my fix, I'd bring stories every week of different things I'd be doing; made up, fanciful, things conjured from my imagination.

I didn't realise the severity of what I was doing and couldn't predict the long-term consequences either. I was even clueless that this behaviour reflected real problems with my mental health, and that I genuinely needed help. I just wanted someone to like me, but what I was doing left me feeling monstrous. Eventually, I withdrew from therapy, went cold turkey, and successfully overcame my addiction to lying. However, while I left the lies behind, they never left me, and I could never have guessed just how far they would follow me, and how much damage they would cause.

Meanwhile, everyone at school had long since gone back to treating me the way they always did. But they wouldn't be making fun of me soon, not when they found out that, Matthew, the dreamy new guy at school that all the girls wanted, had chosen me. He was so good looking, right off the page of a teen magazine, with golden tanned skin and dark chocolate deep brown eyes that drew you in. He had a charm and wit that made you chuckle uncontrollably, and his smile made you weak at the knees, just like in the movies. He was the prize all the girls wanted to win when he moved into the area and joined Aireville School. But he chose me! The girl the other girls loved to hate. Mum always told me to ignore them, and they would get bored and stop, but it's hard to ignore people making fun of every single thing about you, and eventually you start to believe them. One day it was my shoes they were making fun of, the next day it would be my hair, or my Disney phone case. But it didn't matter anymore because the time for school was over and Matthew and

I were ready to move on with our life. It felt like victory, like at the end of a teen movie, leaving my tormentors behind with the coolest guy in school.

Matthew was already living independently because he couldn't stay with his Gran any longer. So, madly in love with the boy of my fantasies, imagining the most picturesque future together, I moved in with him. Sweet sixteen and living the dream. Mum wasn't happy about it, but she said she'd rather I go with her permission than without. As it turned out, living together soon exposed the rough edges of our differences. Matthew had a lot of friends and stayed out late most nights, while I'm a home bird who's much happier watching a movie on the sofa. Although he asked me to go with him, partying was just not the life I envisaged for us. Matthew and I spoke often about wanting to be a family and, despite our differences, we still saw our relationship as 'loves young dream', and naively began trying for a baby. I locked our ongoing disagreements into a box in my mind where they couldn't sully our dreams.

While we waited to get pregnant, and to appease Matthew's concerns about me spending too much time at home, I agreed to return to singing; something that had always been a great joy for me. It is the only thing I've ever done that nobody has judged me badly for or picked on me about. Singing is when I feel truly myself. Singing takes me to my happy place and it has been a constant in my life. I've sung in choirs, performed in plays, at local fairs, and I was even the singer in the school band. I'd also sung a few times at a local club, something arranged by a friend of Mum's, called Darren, who arranged the music, and would partner me with another girl. I contacted Darren and was pleased when he invited me to sing again.

I went to Darren's house for rehearsals where I met his new girlfriend, who was to be my singing partner, Janelle, who had moved in with Darren, along with her children who often watched our rehearsals. Over the first few rehearsals I got to know most of the family, particularly her eldest son, Jason. Although he lived elsewhere, he was always there visiting his mum. He was scruffy, like Shaggy from Scooby Doo, minus the dog, and with long red hair that he always wore tied back with an old cap over the top. His clothes were baggy, faded and torn. I got that for some people this was a kind of style, but for Jason it came across as a lack of effort or care in his appearance. Once I saw him reach for a box on the very top of the kitchen units, a stretch even for him, and his top lifted to show his pale and skeletal stomach, and I remember grimacing and looking away.

As the weeks went by we had more and more rehearsals during the week and I also went to practice during the afternoons, and Jason always seemed to be there. We'd started to get to know each other quite well and quickly became friends. Eventually, very little rehearsing got done because it was lovely just to have a friend to share time with. When we weren't at the house together, Jason and I texted each other to keep our conversations going.

What started as something I took on to please Matthew, had now turned into something that he didn't like me doing. He'd noticed the constant texting between me and Jason and thought that Jason liked me as more than just a friend. I thought Matthew was making issues where there were none because we'd been arguing so much at the time about his friends. I'd told him how he acted like a different person when they were around, and not the person I knew and loved. Clearly, because I didn't like his friends, he had chosen not to like mine. With nobody else to talk to about this, I shared it with Jason, who decided that Matthew was just jealous that I had something good in my life with singing and meeting new people. According to Jason, Matthew wanted to keep me to himself.

7

I definitely did not want to lose Matthew over this and promised that if anything started to get weird with Jason, or he showed any signs of liking me, then I would walk away from the singing. A week later, and Matthew and I were out for a meal together, something we'd never done before. I was so happy because this was exactly the kind of romantic thing I imagined us doing when we left school. After our meal, under the candlelight of the restaurant, Matthew's hand reached out with an open box resting on his palm and he asked me to marry him. I said yes!

I thought Jason would be excited for me but instead he began dropping hints about having feelings for me. I could no longer deny to myself that Jason and I had grown close over the past few months, but I said nothing to him and went home. A few hours later, Matthew and I were sat watching TV when my phone beeped to signal I had a new text. It was from Jason and read 'ich Liebe dich'. Although neither Matthew nor I spoke German, we both instinctively new this translated as 'I love you'. Enraged, Matthew demanded I give him the phone. He called Jason, who answered, likely thinking it was me, and Matthew asked him what he was doing sending his fiancée a text telling her he loves her. Matthew demanded Jason meet him in a local car park where they could 'sort this like men' and stormed out. I was petrified because I knew this could go horribly wrong, but in the end, Jason failed to show up and Matthew came home with an ultimatum; I had to choose between him or singing. I chose Matthew.

Chapter Two

CJ

We had been trying to get pregnant for eighteen months without success when, finally, my period was late. I didn't have any other signs, but my cycles were usually like clockwork. Matthew and I made the short walk into town and bought a pregnancy test. While we were out we decided to treat ourselves and eat lunch in a café. Our lives might be about to change, and we wanted to make a day of it. In preparation for taking the pregnancy test I'd drunk a lot of water and I needed to go somewhere to eat that had a bathroom. We chose the Sunwin House café and Matthew ordered while I went to the bathroom.

Once within the privacy of the cubicle, I decided I couldn't wait, and took the pregnancy test. I read the instructions carefully twice, to be sure I was doing it right. I did what I needed to do and replaced the cap on the stick. It was too nerve wracking to watch, so I covered the stick with the instructions sheet and gave it a few minutes. Those few minutes felt like the longest of my life.

I realised it had been four years since I sat in my big sister's bedroom waiting while she was in the family bathroom doing exactly what I was doing now. Lisa was sixteen years old at the time and I sat with her older boyfriend waiting for her to come out and share the result. When she did, it was positive, and she was visibly shaking and asked me to tell Mum. I was only thirteen years old at the time, but I gingerly went downstairs and casually asked Mum what she would say if I told her Lisa was pregnant.

The speed of her reply caught me like a slap, "I'd be very angry, why"?

"No reason, I just wondered", I said and quickly retreated.

Lisa then sent her boyfriend down to do the job and, after what seemed like hours, we heard the living room door open and Mum start up the stairs shouting, "Bloody hell Lisa!" I escaped to my room but pressed my ear against the wall and listened as they talked. Mum asking what Lisa wanted to do, asking if she was happy, then I heard them both crying, which made me cry even though I wasn't even in the room with them. I know Mum probably wished Lisa had waited longer and been more careful, but eventually we were all happy with the new addition to the family and I couldn't imagine our lives without my nephew. Lisa had her baby young and was an amazing mum, and I wanted to be just like her.

I was about to find out if it was my turn to be a young mum. This was a crossroads. One route was to continue down the same road with its monthly disappointments of negative tests. The other route was to a life of being a young parent and living the life we'd dreamed of for eighteen long months. I was shaking as I lifted the instructions and found two lines staring back at me. I was pregnant!

I returned to Matthew, who was sat at our table with our food waiting for me. I could tell he was confused because it was obvious I'd been crying but I was wearing a beaming smile. I showed him the test and his grin lit up the room. We talked excitedly about the baby we'd known about for only a few minutes yet already loved so much, before my mind turned to how I would tell Mum. I already had some idea of how that would go, so before that happened, we enjoyed being the only two people in the world to know about our little jellybean.

The next day I waited outside Lisa's work for her to finish her shift, and when she appeared I blurted out that I was pregnant. She seemed happy, if not a little shocked. I'm not sure anyone expected me to get pregnant at a young age. Most people would have expected me to do things differently, but I had moved out at sixteen and recently got engaged, so I was obviously trying to live my life all at once.

Just as Lisa had asked me to tell Mum about her pregnancy, I asked her to return the favour. It was such a relief when she agreed, but I could see she was as nervous as I had been, even though she got to do it over the phone. I couldn't hear Mum's response and Lisa relayed that although she wasn't overjoyed, she also wasn't angry. At this point Mum had some practice with pregnant teenage daughters, so I imagine it wasn't as much of a shock the second time around. At the end of the day, we spoke over the phone and while her tone was most definitely one of disapproval, her words came tame and soft. After a week or so, when I next saw her and we got the initial shock out of the way, everything went back to normal. It wasn't like we could do anything about it now, and I think seeing how happy I was certainly helped. And my joy at becoming a Mum was obvious to the world.

On the fourth attempt the needle finally went in without my vein collapsing, and the nurse could both extract enough blood and stick the cannula into my arm. My pale, thinning arms were already bruised and swollen from the three previous failed attempts to get this done. Before the pregnancy I'd never been in hospital overnight before. Now I'd been here several times over the last few weeks. At first staying only two days, then three, and then four. Each hospital admission was longer and the time I spent at home shorter.

I was diagnosed with hyperemesis gravidarum. In short, it's when your morning sickness becomes something much worse. I was sick all day, all night, and every single day. It started when I was about six weeks pregnant and by week eight I'd had my very first hospital stay. I was severely dehydrated because I couldn't eat, and when I forced myself it just came back up, so I was on constant intravenous fluids. I already had a needle phobia and the constant blood tests, and cannulas hadn't helped, so when they started talking about putting a feeding tube in it scared the beejesus out of me. I kept hearing, 'if you're scared of needles, how are you going to give birth', which seemed both inappropriate and patronising in equal measure. Since developing hyperemesis gravidarum and being unable to keep food down, I was losing weight when I should have been gaining. Still, I was grateful that the baby was taking what it needed from my reserves and growing well.

Because hyperemesis gravidarum is uncommon, it was always a toss-up as to how understanding the medical staff behaved towards me, which meant my care wasn't always consistently caring. Often I was accused of doing it to myself, or electing not to eat to stay thin, which was ridiculous. I loathed when the disbelieving consultants came, and I had nobody with me. My voice was too quiet, too insignificant to be heard. I was still too young to be taken seriously. If the consultant decided they'd done all they could for me, I'd be discharged and sent home, only to need to be re-admitted a couple of days later.

Pregnancy was so far from what I thought it would be. Where was my glow? Where was the peaceful, magical time that you're meant to have as you grow the most precious thing in life? We enjoyed a few blissful weeks and then, just as Mum was getting used to the idea of me having a baby, the hyperemesis gravidarum meant everything abruptly changed. At home, it was starting to affect me and Matthew being able to spend time together, because even the smell of his aftershave and shower gel were making me sick. Also, because he wasn't always able to get to the hospital, we were together much less often. I knew he'd started to see his friends again; I was questioning if he even wanted to come and see me, or if it was just easier for him to stay with his friends and forget about the burden of an ill fiancée. We hadn't spoken about the baby much since I got sick. It was hard to even remember I was pregnant some days, through the agony of a torn oesophagus and dry retching and feeling too frail to even get to the bathroom.

Our rent agreement stated that we had to let the landlord know of any children in the house. When we called to tell them we were pregnant, they asked us to leave. We were in a one-bedroom property, so we needed to move eventually, but this was not the best time. I was so sick that I ended up going back into the hospital, leaving Matthew the responsibility of finding a house and moving us. The Council wouldn't help us until we were homeless, and we couldn't take the risk of deliberately putting ourselves in that position. I couldn't focus while being in hospital. I was just trying to find the mental energy to make it through each day of never-ending sickness. We had our gender scan, with Matthew taking time off work to be there, and learned we were having a boy! We were both so excited, and although neither of us had a preference, I secretly think that Matthew may have wanted a boy.

Despite wearing four layers, I was freezing, and only reluctantly climbed out from under the duvet to walk gently and slowly to the bathroom. We were in the only house Matthew could find that would accept a young couple with no money and who needed assistance to pay the rent. It was now autumn 2005, and the weather had turned much cooler. The house was old and draughty and impossible to heat. I managed to get to and from the bathroom and back into bed, but the physical movement came at a price and I vomited into my bucket. Crying with self-pity, I put my hand on my stomach and thought about our little boy. He gave me the strength I needed to get through this. I'd been told that, since the sickness hadn't improved by that point it would likely last until the end of the pregnancy. It was hell just thinking about the months of illness still ahead of me. A seeming eternity of horror still to be endured before the moment of great happiness with our baby.

Matthew was spending so much time with his friends, even when I wasn't in the hospital, that I rarely saw him. I asked if we were okay, but it was never a conversation he seemed to want to have. I knew he'd been working hard with his apprenticeship, but he still stayed out late each night. It was clear that he needed the time away, some respite, something he could find but I couldn't, but I didn't begrudge him that because I wasn't much company. We still hadn't spoken about the baby very much; the severity of my sickness was much more than either of us could ever have imagined and it had shown that Matthew and I weren't as strong as I thought. I needed him here beside me, I needed him to look after me, but it was a lot for a newly 18-year-old guy to take on. I was scared that I didn't recognise my fiancé anymore. Yet, I had a baby to fight for, and I knew he would bring love back into our lives, so I locked these doubts in the box in my mind.

I'd been back in hospital for another week. More needles, more intravenous fluids that provided only a temporary benefit, only addressing the symptoms of hyperemesis, never touching the cause. I was being discharged but couldn't reach Matthew and feared going home to find he'd gone. It was such a relief when Mum dropped me off to find him there. But it was short lived because he was only there to tell me it was all too much, that he wasn't ready to be a dad, and that he wanted us to take a break. He asked me to leave.

I called Mum and briefly told her what had happened and asked if I could come home. I had nowhere else to go. Matthew ran around and packed some things for

14

me. He seemed eager to get me out of the house, but I could also see how broken he appeared, this was hard for him too. I wished I had the energy to be the fiancée he needed me to be, but I didn't. Mum pulled up outside and I ran out, so she didn't come in and hurl verbal abuse at Matthew. I know the last thing Matthew needed was to answer to Mum. I got in the car and we drove away. I never went back to that house.

But I did go back to Matthew. After spending a miserable Christmas at home with my Mum and Step-Dad, the doorbell rang on New Year's Eve and it was Matthew, he'd come bearing gifts. One was for me, a pink pearl heart shaped necklace with a silver chain. It made me cry because other than our son, it's the most beautiful and thoughtful gift he'd ever given me. The other gift was for our baby. A perfect set of Peter Rabbit themed sterling silver baby keepsakes, a trinket box, and a bangle. I was crying even more because I knew he'd lovingly gone out and thought about what to get me and the baby. With time apart, Matthew realised he'd missed me and wanted to give it another go; he wanted to try to be a dad. After that tiny hiccup, that part in the film where it all goes wrong, we were on track now for our happy ending.

It hadn't been a smooth road, but we were together again, which is what mattered the most. The Council told us that since I was now heavily pregnant they could put us into emergency accommodation, which was a local hotel on the outskirts of town. I remained bedbound with hyperemesis while Matthew found us an idyllic, one-bedroom apartment with a balcony overlooking the canal, in the centre of town. Finally, we were in a stable home, with furniture and everything for the baby ready to go, and we were just over a month away from meeting our son.

Unsurprisingly, I ended up back in the hospital again. I was hoping this stay and round of intravenous fluids would be enough to see me through to the end of the pregnancy and I was looking forward to being discharged, but our baby had different plans. I was 35 weeks and one day pregnant and it was show time; it was hard not to freak out!

Eventually I was moved into the delivery room, I had Matthew there doing a great job of holding my hand and staying at the top of the bed, where I wanted him. The intensity of the pain was getting worse very quickly and I realised that labour was no joke. I hit the big 10cm, so began the pushing stage, which for me was quick and only took a few tries. CJ was born at 2.24am after just five hours of labour, though it seemed much longer. Thankfully it wasn't the slow labour I was expecting from Mum's terrifying warnings, although compared to the torture that a pregnancy with hyperemesis feels like, labour was nothing in comparison. Labour was the journeys end, the pathway to finally getting to see and hold the little miracle I had fought hard for through eight months of hell. When CJ was born, they held him up so I could have a quick look and he promptly christened the joyous moment by doing a little wee on me, much to everyone's amusement. Matthew cut the cord through his happy tears and they took CJ to be cleaned and checked.

I was cleaned up too and finally ready to hold our little boy for the first time. They passed him to me wrapped in a plain white blanket with a little white hat covering his dark hair. His eyes were closed, and he was making sweet baby noises as he slept. My life felt complete with CJ in it. I was exhausted but totally whole. It was as though I'd always been walking around with a part of me missing, and CJ was that missing part that finally found me. I was so in love with him. An unconditional love that nobody else in the entire world could give me, and I couldn't give to anyone else. A mother's love.

The most special moment of my life was when everyone left. Suddenly, CJ and I were the only two people in the world. Holding him close, I drank in his newborn baby smell and I spoke to him for the first time, mother to son. "Do you know the fight I've had just to get you here baby? I fought so hard through all that sickness and you are worth every bit of it," I told him proudly. Then I told him the story of how he came to be, "Once upon a time I wished upon a star from my bedroom window for you to come into my life, and now you're here I love you so much already and I'll love you forever." I continued telling him all we were going to do together, "There are so many things that I want to show you, the ducks in the canal, the park, and the swings where you can play when you're older. We're gonna go on trains and boats, maybe even planes. I'll show you the whole world if you want me to. I promise I will always keep you safe, I'll be there to take care of you. It's just gonna be me and you together, against the world. You will always be my one and only. My sunshine." And then I sang the song 'You are my sunshine', to him as he drifted off to sleep and it truly felt like everything in my life had fallen into place perfectly.

Chapter Three
Knight in Shining Armour

For the first four weeks after bringing CJ home we existed in our beautiful new baby bubble. For days on end Matthew, CJ and I would snuggle on the sofa just watching the world go by. We tackled night-time feeds, dirty nappies and even colic like we were learning to walk again. Babies don't come with instructions, but we were in it together and it was blissful. Watching Matthew hold CJ, smiling at him and talking to him about anything and everything, it was clear Matthew adored CJ, and it was lovely to witness those special moments, but that didn't last.

Matthew went back to work and over time, each day Matthew returned home it was like he left a little of himself somewhere else. Instead of the attentive father and fiancé, he was grumpy, tired, and sometimes he wouldn't come home at all because he'd stay with his friends enjoying some time to himself. After preparing his tea one evening after work, we were in the kitchen as CJ slept in the other room. Matthew ate and then got up from the table and went to leave the room. I asked him to clean his plate and he said, "If you're cleaning up after CJ, you can clean up after me." In that moment, when those words hit me, I knew the path we were on.

Matthew had a day off and I needed to talk to him, so Lisa took CJ for the day. My heart was thumping as I started a conversation that I imagined would be the beginning of the end. I didn't want to do this. I loved him so much, but I knew I wasn't in love with him anymore. If I'm honest, I don't think I had been for a very long time. What was about to happen would break Matthew's heart and there was no easy way to do it. I just had to jump right in.

I pointed out that he'd been out late with his friends a lot leaving me and CJ on our own, and that it felt like he didn't want to be with us anymore. He seemed shocked and looked defensive, but before even opening his mouth to speak, his face changed to one of defeat and he admitted that he didn't think he was ready for this. My heart jerked on hearing the familiar 'I'm not ready for this'. It was like a knife to the heart that, now CJ is here he still thought he couldn't do this. I'd seen him with CJ, he was better than he thought, but I didn't know how to convince him. I wanted to beg him to stop acting like this, I wanted desperately to be the couple we were in those first few weeks after bringing CJ home. But it was pointless. I don't think either of us were truly in the relationship anymore, and one of us needed to notice.

I told him I felt like a single parent and that I didn't think we loved each other anymore. "I love you!" came his reply, but it was said defensively and unconvincingly, like an automated response. I told him I love him too, but I wasn't in love anymore. I said I would always love him because he gave me CJ, but I didn't want to be with him anymore.

He was upset and angry and our talk turned to argument, with us both in tears by the end. Matthew packed some of his things and left. When Lisa returned with CJ, I shared what happened, and she let me talk it out. Then she left and I got CJ ready for bed and sat in the flat alone with my thoughts. Being with Matthew felt right, and it still did in some ways. Maybe it was just the timing, maybe this was the part in our story where we go find ourselves and grow as people, and one day we would realise we are meant to be, and we'd find our way back to each other. Maybe instead of the end, this was more of an interlude.

19

Only a week after Matthew left, someone else entered my life. We sat looking at each other, and I didn't want her here. If people knew, what would they think? That I'm an unfit mum, that's what they'd think. Nobody has Social Services involved for being a good parent. This was our first meeting, and my guard was well and truly up. As she came in, she looked around the room and took in CJ's cot adorned with teddies and Winnie the Pooh toys and his chest of drawers with one drawer broken. It happened during our last move and hadn't been a financial priority to get a new one, and being single now, it was even further down my list. She walked over to the sofa and sat down, sorting through her big black bag to find her notebook and a pen, all the better to write down her judgements.

I placed CJ on the floor where he happily played with his toys and smiled endearingly at this new visitor. As she prepared herself to talk to me, I tried to gauge how this was going to go by how she held herself. She didn't look too dissimilar to me, though older, she had dark brown long hair tied up in a pristine ponytail. Her eyes are almost black, much darker than mine. She was dressed in a full black outfit, professional but not in a way that alienated the stay-at-home mum. She had a nice smile, one she offered as soon as I opened the door, though I didn't yet know whether this was from politeness or if she was genuine. When I greeted her at the door she introduced herself as Vicky.

I sat with my hands locked between my knees to hide the shaking. I was still upset we'd even been referred to them. When the Health Visitor had last visited, my back had gone out the night before; maybe I'd slept funny, I'm not sure. It was difficult for me to move around and so I did the best I could by gathering everything I needed into the centre of the room and spent the day there with CJ, only moving for necessities like the toilet or CJ's bottles. I had his toys, his nappies and changing mat. I had blankets for his naps, everything was within reach and I played with him the same way I did every day. The Health Visitor was concerned when I told her I was now single and that I was struggling. I had also been feeling quite low for a while with the pressure of daily life, so she referred me to Social Services because she felt I was young and vulnerable. It was a bitter and hard pill to swallow to think you're doing the best you can, but someone else decided it's not quite good enough, and you need more support.

We went through some of the basic questions about CJ's age and how was he doing developmentally. Then she asked more personal questions about me and my mental health and asked for permission to view my medical records. However, after the formalities, we talked like two people simply getting to know each other. Vicky adored CJ and played with him throughout. I made her a brew and we put a plan in place for her to come and see me a couple of times a week, just for support purposes. As she left, it felt like she understood that the biggest thing I was missing right now was company, someone to talk to. I breathed a sigh of relief when the initial meeting passed with no mention of me being a terrible mum, or that I was doing something wrong.

During the last year of my relationship with Matthew, lacking attention while pregnant and wanting someone to talk to, my thoughts would drift to Jason. I wondered how he was and what he was doing. In a 'grass is always greener' kind of way I imagined how life might have been, had I chosen him instead. Then, when CJ was born my life revolved around him and I stopped fantasising as much about what could have been and focused and what I had right in front of me. Now I was single those thoughts of Jason were returning.

When CJ was two months old, to give me a break, Lisa took him for a few days. While I was alone I took the chance to reach out to Jason, to see if he wanted to catch up. He texted me saying he'd like to see me, so we arranged to meet at Darren's house and then go out for the day. As he opened the door, I didn't immediately recognise him, he had changed so much. I couldn't help but smile. Jason' hair was now its original mousey brown, short and styled into spikes, and it completely changed his appearance. He was wearing a short sleeved, blue patterned shirt with fitted dark blue jeans and smart, polished black shoes. I was suddenly glad that I too put effort into my outfit. The feelings I had once had for Jason came rushing back, and now I was also physically attracted to him, which was new. What was once just his personality drawing me in, was now much more of a full package. Though looks had never been the most important thing to me, I could appreciate that Jason looked much better now.

We decided to meet on Jason' birthday, and went to a local market town for lunch, with his mum joining us. It certainly didn't make for best first date, but I understood why she wanted to see him on his birthday. His mum and I were civil, not that I'd be anything else, and Jason and I soon made our way back to my flat. We caught up over drinks while watching television and I told him all about CJ. Jason told me what he'd been doing in the last year, focusing on trying to find work so much that he hadn't been seeing anyone romantically. We sat in my living room talking into the early hours.

As the first signs of daylight touched the curtains, I realised neither of us had slept, so invited him to sleep on the sofa while I caught a few hours of sleep in my room. When we woke up, Jason made us both a drink and cleared the kitchen while I took a shower. He seemed very at home. I ran across the road to my favourite bakery and returned with bacon sandwiches for breakfast and we continued our chat from the night before. Not yet having run out of things to say, our conversations were effortless, but it had been a while since I had anyone to talk to like this and I clearly needed it.

I told him that me and Matthew had only recently broken up and why that was, and he let me have a cry on his shoulder about what went so wrong. I was mostly upset for CJ these days, that he wasn't going to get the two-parent upbringing I wanted for him. Jason exclaimed that he couldn't wait to meet CJ. It was obvious that we enjoyed each other's company, given how long we'd just sat and intensely stared at each other as we poured out our lives. Admitting our mutual feelings for one another, we floated the idea of being together, followed by lots of flirting into a second night together, and he just never left.

CJ was finally home, and I hugged him for a solid hour to remind my body what it felt like, and what I'd been missing. I'm sure he'd grown while he was gone. I introduced CJ to Jason, who was so good with him. Jason was obviously a natural with children, likely from having so many younger siblings. He took a real shine to CJ and we spent the following few days just hanging out at the flat together, getting to grips with our new normal. Life just felt so easy with Jason. It never once occurred to me that this was rushing things. There weren't many guys who would want to be with someone with a baby, but Jason did. He just seemed to fit, and he treated CJ like his own, he even called himself Daddy when talking to CJ, and he did so much around the house without me even asking, he barely let me lift a finger. Jason was my knight in shining armour, come to rescue the damsel in distress.

After some respite, I was being sick again and I couldn't stop. I had nothing but air left inside me, and I was gasping for breath and struggling with the pain from the burning on the inside of my throat that had been torn to shreds by the acid in my vomit. I regretted not putting myself on to some form of contraception and thinking a condom would suffice. Yet, here I was, only a month after we started dating, and me and Jason were pregnant, and hyperemesis had returned with a vengeance. This time it started sooner and was more relentless than the first time. I was tormented by the fact that I could barely hold CJ for more than a minute before Jason needed to take him away; partly so CJ didn't see me like that and partly to avoid me getting worse through the physical strain of holding him. A visit to the doctor brought no solace to this familiar hell. Only the knowledge that this illness could, and likely would, always happen with any pregnancy I had, a fact that I hadn't known before that day.

Jason was initially excited to become a dad, then when I started getting sick so soon it became difficult for him to watch. I couldn't get out of bed and most days could barely keep my eyes open. I didn't see CJ unless Jason brought him to me, but when he did I couldn't play with him without vomiting from the movement. It was torture.

Social Services came for a routine visit and Vicky wasn't happy that I was pregnant and unable to look after CJ, though having Jason there seemed to curb her disapproval. She told me bluntly that I needed to consider my options because they may need to be more involved if I became ill to the point where I couldn't take care of CJ myself, which was the current situation, or would be had it not been for Jason. As much as I truly didn't want to, both Jason and I knew that I was too sick, and I couldn't keep on going like this. After CJ was asleep, Jason came to sit with me, and we talked about our future. We agreed that the best thing for all of us, was for me to have an abortion. We sourced a clinic and Lisa took CJ for the day while Jason and I made the journey there. When we returned, no longer pregnant, I felt empty and utterly ashamed of myself. I spent a lot of days crying, but I couldn't deny that it was a relief to be able to hold and play with my son again. Striving to bounce back, I ignored the guilt so I could focus on CJ and locked any doubt and all the pain in the box in my mind.

Jason and I arrived back at the flat after going out for a few hours. Matthew had CJ that day for the first time since we split. As we went through the door to the stairway of the flat, I looked up to see Matthew sitting on the top step with CJ in his lap. Flustered and mid-panic, I froze. For the last few weeks, Matthew and I had been chatting and attempting to be civil so that he could see CJ and spend time with him. When Matthew had visited to pick up some of his things, I took the opportunity to tell him that I was with Jason. The news wasn't easy for him to take, but for CJ's sake we tried to get past it and to avoid any awkward confrontations, we arranged that when Matthew came to pick CJ up that Jason wouldn't be there. Now, there we all stood in the same narrow, barely lit stairway.

Through the strained atmosphere that teetered on the edge of an out and out fight, I noticed CJ was red and puffy; he'd clearly been crying quite a lot, which wasn't like him. He hadn't seen Matthew for several weeks and I wondered if CJ was no longer comfortable around him. Breaking the tension, I asked why they were back so early, and Matthew told me he was unable to get CJ to settle and stop crying, so he felt that it was for the best to bring him home.

As we walked up the stairs and I opened the door to the flat, I noticed both Matthew and Jason doing their best to pretend the other wasn't there. Neither of them raised their heads or looked in the other's direction and I was glad they were doing this for CJ's sake. Jason retreated to the bedroom to allow Matthew and I space to talk. I asked what happened to make CJ cry, and he said he'd just been around town with him, then back to where he was staying, and that CJ had been fine. Then he became unsettled for no reason and was inconsolable. By this point CJ was settled in his pram and seemed tired, so I let him sleep and Matthew left.

Like a rabbit peering out from their burrow to check for danger, Jason popped his head out from the bedroom door, and I gave him the 'all clear' to come out. He seemed scared, but relieved to have gotten through his first encounter with Matthew unscathed.

Half an hour later I heard CJ stirring and I went to see him. His eyes were weary, and I noticed a small red mark on the side of his face. Was he still blotchy from crying? I assumed it was likely just a mark from where he'd rested his head while sleeping. I got them all the time from the creases on my pillow, or if I fell asleep on my hand. Noticing my puzzled expression, Jason came over and I pointed to the side of CJ's head. Jason took a closer look and I watched as he pressed the side of CJ's head, looked into his eyes, and raised his head. Jason was first aid trained and it showed; I was impressed. I had no idea what he was doing but he turned to me and said there was nothing to worry about. He explained that when he touched the side of CJ's head and he didn't react, and it didn't bother him, this meant there was nothing to worry about. Jason was adamant that CJ would have reacted if it hurt him. His calming tone reassured me, and we carried on with our evening as a family. Naively, I never gave it a second thought. I wouldn't know until it was too late that trusting Jason was one huge mistake.

Chapter Four
Ten Pence Piece

I remember looking down at the floor as I retraced my own footsteps on the vinyl floor for what felt like hours on end. We were waiting for the doctor to come in and give us some news, any news. I know I was anxious, but I was also angry that it was taking them so long just to tell us that nothing was wrong with CJ. I felt silly for even bringing him to the hospital now. I thought I was just being over-protective and blowing this whole thing out of proportion.

After Matthew left on the Saturday, Jason, CJ, and I shared a pretty average weekend together with nothing of note happening. In fact, it was so normal I don't even remember it. Had I known what would happen I'd have soaked in every second of that weekend. On the Monday morning Jason left early to attend a training course the Job Centre had sent him on, as he was currently unemployed. He got CJ dressed and ready for the day and I came to say goodbye and give CJ his breakfast. I sat him down on my knee in front of the double patio doors and as the morning light shone on his face I noticed a small, light purple bruise to the right side of CJ's head. It was about the size of a ten pence piece, directly over the temple area, in the same place the red mark had been just a few days earlier; but that had faded and disappeared by the time he woke up the next day, and we hadn't noticed anything since then. I couldn't be sure if this were related or not, but I also knew I hadn't seen CJ hit his head.

If Jason had been at home I would have likely asked him what to do, especially since he'd told me he was first aid trained. But he wasn't there and so, out of an abundance of caution, I phoned the Health Visitor to ask what to do about the bruise and whether I should be worried. I hadn't done this before, and I was still very much in the 'please hold my hand and tell me what to do' stage of motherhood.

The Health Visitor explained that it was probably nothing to be too concerned about, but I should take him to A&E to be safe, especially as I didn't know how the bruise came to be there. Since we didn't drive and the only family member who did was on holiday, I rang our social worker, Vicky, and relayed what the Health Visitor had said, and she offered to take me to the hospital. I knew I would have to call Jason because he wouldn't like me to go to the hospital without telling him. He insisted on coming and left his course and was home before the Social Worker arrived. He had a quick look at the bruise and said straight away that he thought it was nothing, I remember him not being overly happy with the fact that I called the Social Worker, but I didn't see that I had another choice.

We went to A&E but were soon sent to the children's ward to get things processed a little quicker. On arriving on the ward, we were taken into a room beside the nurses' station. The room was small with a cream metal cot in the middle that seemed more like a cage and not something I wanted to put CJ in, but I didn't have a choice, by this time he was tired and needed a nap. The walls were painted bright green, almost turquoise, with a cartoon sea themed border around the top of the room. One of the walls had a large glass window that overlooked the nurses' station, which of course meant they could see everything we were doing too, and it very quickly felt like being in a fishbowl.

Over the next few hours, they gave CJ all the tests possible: ears, eyes, listening to his chest etc. He didn't get to sleep for long, but he was so well behaved given the circumstances. We were told after the routine tests that they wanted to give him a CT scan. As he was only five months old though, they needed to put him to sleep to do it as he would need to stay still. We consented but began to feel it was becoming excessive for such a 'barely there' bruise. Although I was grateful for the care and thoroughness of tests, I was getting the sense that something was a little off. I felt like there was something that I wasn't being told and it was making me nervous. I tried to shake it off as just being in a bad mood from being stuck in a small room for such a long time.

There's something particularly upsetting about a child when they're sick. They seem smaller somehow. I remember when they wheeled CJ down for his scan. We couldn't go with him and seeing him being driven away as he slept through the anaesthesia felt like handing over the reins a little; a feeling I hated. All of these tests were things that I couldn't do for him, and there was a potential they could hurt him, and I had no control, and I couldn't help him in that moment. It's a terrifying and vulnerable position for a parent to be in.

When CJ came back it was like nothing had happened, he was back to his old happy-go-lucky self after having a good rest. He was always such a happy baby. Though I thought nothing would be wrong with him, I was still nervous to get the results, so we could get out of the hospital and go home. It was late afternoon, and we were still waiting for answers. We'd had various nurses and doctors coming in to ask us to explain why we were there and asking us several times how CJ got the bruise. I didn't know how many more times I could go over the same things and kept telling them that I didn't know what caused the bruise. It was like they were waiting for us to give them a different answer, one they would accept, like the one we were giving was incorrect.

So, there I was pacing the floor back and forth, retracing my own steps when then doctor came into the room with some news, finally. I was relieved thinking this meant we'd be able to take CJ home. I looked up and noticed a stern expression on the doctor's face. He seemed serious. I immediately had a lump in my throat and my heart was racing, realising something was wrong, very wrong. I'd like to say I could remember what was said word for word, but this moment is a blur to me now, something maybe I locked away because it was the moment that everything changed. The doctor proceeded to explain that the scan had shown that CJ was suffering from a subdural hematoma on his right-side temple. This meant that he was bleeding between his skull and his brain. He confirmed it wasn't large, but the presence of this kind of bleed indicated that CJ had suffered a significant injury, likely one that would have been obvious to us at the time. We were told that CJ would have been crying for some time and would have been inconsolable, maybe he'd have been out of sorts and unlike himself afterwards. I know I heard all of this, but I don't think any of it sunk in for a long while.

We were told that nothing needed to be done and he wasn't in any danger medically, so we didn't need to be worried. They would need to keep him in for observation and to get to the bottom of how the injury happened. It was hard for me to believe what they were saying because I hadn't seen CJ be hurt in any way. He hadn't fallen and there hadn't been a time over the last few days when he was crying. I was so confused. We asked how long it would be before he could come home, but they couldn't tell us at that time. The doctor then explained to us that this was a serious injury, one they had to report because it could only be caused by a large amount of force. 'Blunt force trauma', he said, I did hear that part. They used so much jargon when they talk, sometimes it was hard to know if what he was saying was good. I definitely hadn't fully comprehended all I was told. I remember looking at CJ and just crying. I think I was half crying knowing something had happened to my little boy and I'd had no idea, and half because my head was just full of a tonne of information that I was struggling to understand. The fact the doctor said we would have known when this happened, yet there wasn't a single time I could pinpoint when CJ had been the way he described. He was a placid baby; we would have remembered this kind of thing. I was so upset, and I felt like they had to be wrong.

Vicky pulled us aside after I calmed down and said that due to the nature of the injury Social Services would have to investigate, but she didn't want us to worry right now, and said to focus on CJ getting better. I didn't have space in my head to worry, all I could do was wrack my brain trying to figure this all out. Jason and I both kept thinking over and over whether CJ had recently bumped his head or dropped a toy on his head.

I was never given the opportunity to stay in hospital with CJ, so I had to leave him there alone. We spent the entire night doing just as we had at the hospital and that's when Jason reminded me of what happened with Matthew at the weekend when he brought CJ home early. I laughed it off at first, Matthew adored CJ he'd never hurt him and if anything happened he would have told me. But Jason kept pressing it and wouldn't let it go. He said we should tell the doctors and Social Services, and I reluctantly agreed. Jason had already decided what happened. He said it explained the whole situation.

The next day I got a call from the Social Services manager telling me I needed to come into the office before I went to see CJ at the hospital. I had to go alone. I guessed they needed to talk over what was happening with CJ. I walked into manager's office and the manager and a colleague were both sat behind the desk in front of me. The room was small, and the blind was closed, making the room quite dark. There was a public footpath right outside the window, so I imagined it was for privacy reasons. I knew the manager vaguely, as she was the mother of an old classmate of mine but there was no chit chat, no pleasantries, and they didn't ask after CJ. I assumed they already knew and had been in contact with the hospital themselves.

In no uncertain terms, I was immediately told that CJ wasn't coming home with me when he was able to leave the hospital. The manager said Social Services were in the process of assigning a foster family for CJ to stay with, and they were immediately applying for custody to be removed from myself and Matthew, with a view to doing an assessment of our parenting abilities. She explained that if these were found to be unsatisfactory, CJ would be permanently removed from our care and placed for adoption. She also stated that they had spoken to the police about the injury, and they would be in touch to speak to me soon. I was no longer allowed to be with CJ alone, even in the hospital, nor could any of my family be alone with him.

I remember feeling like I couldn't breathe. Like the ground had fallen beneath me.

"You can't do this; I haven't done anything wrong. He's my son I love him", I pleaded.

No emotions registered on their faces, there was no offer of a tissue and no comfort provided. My heart had physically broken, and these women were so cold in the face of a young mother who had been told the worst news of her life. I was barely eighteen years old; my son was in the hospital and I was completely alone, yet these two adult Social Workers needed to come in a pair, but the vulnerable and already distraught young girl had to be by herself. A river of tears gushed from my eyes, I was begging them not to do this, I had never felt such desperation, but I couldn't win. I was told I could go, and I stood up to leave with very little communication between us. I almost fell to my knees when I stood, it felt like the walls were closing in on me and I wished I'd had someone there to catch me. As I walked home I remember keeping my head down because I couldn't look anyone in the face. I kept wondering what people might be thinking as they saw me walking through town with what I knew would be a very red and puffy face. I counted the steps until I was home.

Jason cried when I told him what they had said, but with anger in his tears. He started to raise his voice, yelling that they couldn't do this, and they had no proof. He continued to say it shouldn't be happening and they should be talking to Matthew, since he's the one that did it. Even though we didn't know that Jason' mind was made up on the subject. I was so beside myself I just went along with it. I just want to see my baby and be with him. Our Social Worker came later that day and took us to the hospital. When we got there, it was like everyone was looking at us with judgement in their eyes, like they all knew our business and had decided that I had hurt CJ. I sat in the room and hugged CJ under the watchful eye of our Social Worker, and I broke down. I just wanted my Mum, but she was out of the country on holiday.

Everything was so surreal; it was so far removed from the life we'd been living even a week earlier. The following few days CJ remained in the hospital even though doctors had confirmed the bleeding had stopped, because Social Services were yet to assign a foster family. I kept thinking the doctors would come to us and say they'd made a huge mistake, but I was thankful that CJ was better and had no permanent damage. Jason was at the hospital with me every single day, he never left my side. He spoke to the doctors with me, and to Social Services. He was just as upset about this as I was, feeling the same as I was, crying when I cried and getting angry when

I was at my wits end trying to come to terms with this. Finally, Mum returned from holiday and came straight to the hospital to see CJ. When we hugged, we both cried, and I almost dropped to the floor in her arms. When you're young and you have a mum hug, it takes the pain away and it makes everything better but even my Mum didn't have any power in this situation, nothing could stop this, just as my hugs hadn't made everything right for CJ.

The time came for CJ to be discharged and we had to say goodbye. We weren't allowed to meet the foster carers at that time and had to leave the hospital before CJ was discharged. We arranged for daily contact during the week for a few hours a day. It felt so wrong to leave without him, knowing he was going home with a stranger. When we got home, and walked through the front door, the flat seemed empty. Void of life. I'd had to pack a few of CJ's things for the hospital and they were sent with him to the foster carers house. Some of his stuff was still here though, his toys and clothes were dotted around and had been there since the day he went into hospital. I fell to the floor, I didn't have the strength to stand anymore, his things only reminded me of happier times and my heart yearned for him. I couldn't help but wonder if he would ever come home again.

Chapter Five

Assessment

It was so hard being at home without CJ. I felt empty not being able to tuck him in at night, not feeding him, changing him, and bathing him, without him I felt like I had no purpose. And yet, I was so filled with shame and horror at the circumstances. This kind of thing didn't happen to people like me. I'd never been in trouble with the law, never hurt anyone, I was never a problem child, I wouldn't say boo to a goose and yet I was being suspected of hurting the only person in this world that I would have died to protect. I came from a normal, fairly put together family. We never had any involvement with Social Services growing up and we had always been such a happy family. If I hadn't been so heartbroken, I'd have been utterly ashamed of the dishonour I felt I'd brought on this family. I had to keep reminding myself that I didn't do anything wrong because I constantly felt guilty, despite having done nothing wrong myself. I was still trying to come to terms with what had happened to CJ and I was finding it harder to try and figure out how his injury was caused. Other than the time he was with his Dad, he was never far from myself or Jason. We had thought of multiple things that we wanted to ask the doctors about what we believed could have happened, but we hadn't yet had the chance to speak to anyone again. Jason firmly believed Matthew had done something, but secretly I knew he would never do that. I don't think Matthew would have ever knowingly harmed CJ, he adored him just as much as I did, but it was always hard to go against Jason when he was so adamant. It was easier just to let him run with it and keep my own opinions to myself.

I had my first contact with CJ, and I had no idea what to expect. Heading to the Social Services office we were taken to a room with lilac walls and a royal blue carpet. There were soft red seats around the edges of the room. The social worker and myself sat down across from each other as we waited for CJ's foster carer to arrive. I hadn't met them yet; I didn't know where he had been staying or who with and the not knowing had been eating away at me. Was there someone out there thinking they had him because his mum was a horrible child abuser? Had they been told that I didn't do anything? The last thing I wanted was someone looking after him and thinking I was a monster. I hoped he was being treated right, but I didn't want them acting like he was their child because he was mine! Was he with a family and around other kids, having to share the spotlight? He wouldn't be used to that. He must have been so scared, wondering where I was, it pained me to wonder if he thought I'd abandoned him. My mind was in a constant state of worry about him, it was all I could do not to have a break down. Although, I hadn't been eating or sleeping properly so, admittedly, I was struggling.

The door to the room had a window and a latch lock so it locked as it closed. From the inside you had to pull on it to open it, and from the outside, you had to either have a key or someone on the inside had to let you in. CJ was brought into the office by his foster carer, and it was the first time I got to see her. She was an older woman, possibly in her fifties. I worried about this because I stereotypically wondered if she would be able to look after CJ, play with him and meet his needs. As if I somehow thought that she couldn't because she was of an older age. Nobody would have been good enough to look after him, because he should have been with me.

When CJ came into the room it was the first time that I'd seen him in an outfit that I didn't pick out for him in the morning, the first time he was in one of the things I'd bought him, but not decided myself he would wear on that specific day. It was something so simple, yet it was one of the many thoughts that entered my mind on seeing him again. I had missed him so much I spent most of the first contact crying, but I knew I had to try and push past that. The hardest part was that this horrible situation turned seeing my son into a negative event. While I was overjoyed to hold him in my arms again, I was watched constantly and never allowed out of the room with him. We were locked away like prisoners in one room for the entire time we were there. I was seeing him, but he wasn't mine anymore, at least not legally. It made me feel like I shouldn't be around my own son. The environment, the circumstances, and the social worker who sat in the corner of the room watching us like a hawk and taking notes of my actions and behaviour, it was all so painfully unnatural that it was impossible to enjoy seeing CJ in this way. It quickly became something I dreaded doing, instead of eagerly anticipating. I was a nervous wreck.

I didn't know what they expected of me. It was horrible feeling like they were judging my every move. I would pause and overthink every little thing I was doing with CJ. Every now and then I would look up to the social worker writing something. I came to associate them writing with me doing something wrong, at least that's what I told myself. In my head, I felt they wouldn't bother writing it down if I were doing something right, so each time it happened I became more upset and scared. I started to doubt my ability to be a mum, at a time when I already felt like I had let CJ down because he had been hurt and I couldn't protect him. The contact sessions started to chip away at my self-esteem and began destroying me much more than it ever helped.

I arranged for Jason to come to the contact meetings with me, I explained that we were together, and CJ had bonded with him too. Jason had been asking me to do this, as he had been missing CJ terribly and didn't like having to stay at home when I went to see him. He would always come to meet me when contact ended, I suspect this was in the hope of catching a glimpse of CJ. Admittedly, I had become heavily dependent on Jason. My mental health had suffered a lot during the pregnancy, then even more so after Matthew and I split up and subsequently being alone for a little while. It all impacted on me in a way that I didn't want to acknowledge. I had been feeling down, hopeless, and lacking motivation to do even the easiest things. Now I had lost CJ, I began to think there was no point to anything. I could barely sleep, other than through sheer exhaustion. I was eating close to nothing and just not taking care of myself in general. When I wasn't seeing CJ, visiting the solicitor or seeing family, I was at home watching the world pass me by. Jason was doing his best to keep me going, he cancelled his training course to be with me and I just agreed to anything he suggested. I had no self-belief anymore, so I put my trust in him.

By August, I was called to the police station where they questioned me about CJ's injury. I had never been in trouble before, never arrested, never had detention, I was never even grounded as a child! I felt so scared and wasn't coping with the fact that people thought I had hurt CJ. Those closest to me would know I'd never be capable of such a thing, but events like this tend to leak out into the community somehow. People hear rumours and Chinese whispers get started and eventually the story gets manipulated so much and I hated knowing that this was likely happening behind my back. I wished I had some way to prove that I didn't do this. I stopped going out because I couldn't be around anyone through the fear that they felt I was to blame. Even people who didn't know me, I would feel that they somehow knew about it and suspected me.

At the police station, I wasn't kept in a cell, but they had to do the full process of reading rights and offering legal counsel, which I didn't take them up on. I had nothing to hide, so I didn't feel the need. The interview room was cramped and dark. The walls were black and there were no windows. There was no two-way mirror like you see on TV, just a small table and a few chairs. Two officers came into the room with me, and I sat alone. I was nervous, and though I knew I had done nothing wrong; this setting could make the most innocent person feel guilty of something.

The police were very steely when questioning me; repeating the same things over and over as if they felt like there were a certain amount of times before I would give in and confess. It was disconcerting that half the time they would speak softly to me and seem to understand, and it felt like they knew I hadn't done this, but that maybe I knew who did and I could tell them anything. I was in a safe space to tell them. When I repeatedly told them, I hadn't witnessed CJ being injured at all, they flipped their approach and for the other half of the interview they rapid fired questions, with persistence and in a way that even I couldn't even keep up. I could only tell them what I knew to be true. I had absolutely no idea who or what caused CJ's injury. All I knew, with certainty, was that I didn't do it. I could never, and the very suggestion was like someone sticking a knife in my heart and ripping it out of my chest. How do you convince people that you are not the monster that many of them must think you are? All I could do was hope that they saw the innocence in me. Somehow. I was there for several hours going back and forth over the same information again and again. It was draining, especially as I was already severely depleted of energy just by waking up each day without my son.

After a couple of weeks, myself, Jason, and Matthew were all considered suspects and each of us was questioned by the police and Social Services met with me and Matthew individually. However, they couldn't determine who had caused the injury as they had no evidence, so they couldn't charge any of us. Ever since CJ had gone into the hospital Jason had continued with his vendetta against Matthew, firmly believing he was the culprit. In the process of the doctors looking into the scans and tests done on CJ, they determined that the bleed had been cause during a three-day window prior to us bringing him into the hospital. CJ was with me and Jason for the majority of that time, aside from the few hours that Matthew had him. The only other time that I wasn't with CJ over that period was in the early hours of the morning when Jason would get CJ up and dressed for the day while I was asleep.

The first words that came out of Jason' mouth when all of this happened was that Matthew had done it. He told the same thing to Social Services and the police, and I felt I had to go along with it because I couldn't go against what Jason was saying. It was a triangle of blame; I knew I didn't do it but neither did I think Matthew or Jason had done it. I thought we were all innocent but in these circumstances you feel like you almost have to point the finger at someone to save yourself. While I never personally said it was Matthew, I allowed Jason to push forward with his accusations and I wasn't honest about how I truly felt. Something I will forever regret.

Moving forward into assessments and court cases, it very much became 'me and Jason' and Matthew. I felt like I was just along for the ride in some respects. I had a solicitor telling us the best way to tackle this, we had Social Services telling us what to do and what to expect. The Children and Family Court Advisory and Support Service (CAFCASS), as the agency primarily representing the child's best interests in all the hearings, became involved, and I had Jason at home who would near constantly be saying we needed to come up with stories and make sure we were both 'singing from the same hymn sheet'. He was like a man possessed coming up with all sorts of ideas to try and detract from our own culpability. I naively went along with everything he suggested because I had no confidence in myself anymore. It never crossed my mind that we shouldn't have needed to make up stories to free ourselves from blame, because I knew I hadn't done anything. In retrospect, I didn't have the right person by my side to give me the support that could have built me up, instead of knocking me down and leading me down the wrong path. It was like filling a bathtub with a dripping tap, it took me too long to realise I was slowly drowning.

A few weeks after being told by the police that they couldn't charge me, I was told by Social Services that I would starting an assessment whereby I would go to the foster carer's home and act as if I had full responsibility for CJ for the day. I was to get him up out of bed and ready for the day; giving him his breakfast, choosing his clothes, and packing some things to take with us to a nearby purpose-made flat. Two social workers shadowed me all day as I went about caring for CJ as I would at home. I was given about a weeks' notice of the assessment but, as I hadn't been offered any support after CJ was removed from my care, I struggled to look after myself and had become physically and emotionally fragile. Consequently, I worried that I might struggle to care for CJ under such circumstances but when I tried to explain, and ask for help, I was told to push past it for CJ. Yet I didn't have the ability to do that, I didn't know how.

When I started the assessment, I found out that CJ was actually staying incredibly close to where we lived. It was hard to know he had been so close all that time. I had to go to the foster carer's house in the morning, a stranger's house, unfamiliar territory. I didn't really do well around other people's houses, a quirk I'd had since I was little, although I'm sure anyone would feel out of place under these circumstances. I was incredibly anxious being in someone else's home, but I did the best I could and arrived at 6am, as instructed, in time to get CJ up and out of his cot.

I quickly realised that CJ was a very different baby to the one I'd left in the hospital almost four months ago. Although I had seen him during contact, his food and bottles were all prepared beforehand, and all I had to do was heat them. During the assessment I was expected to make his meals from scratch, which was totally new for me. I had no idea how to do that, I didn't get to learn it slowly as he weaned, I was thrown in the deep end under the very watchful eyes of two social workers, and judged for not knowing how to do it, and they didn't offer any kind of assistance. They weren't there to help, they were there to judge.

With maturity and hindsight, I sincerely wish I'd made more effort to actively stay on top of CJ's care needs. Even though he was on my mind every second of the day when I wasn't with him, it was like I stopped learning how to care for him once he was gone. I didn't have the wisdom to keep track of his development for when he came home, and I paid for this during the assessment. I suppose, when he was taken away, a part of me gave up before the fight had even begun. Part of me believed I deserved to have him taken because even though I didn't cause the injury, I also didn't protect him. There was so much playing on my mind, so much that felt so out of my control, that I didn't fight as hard as I could or should have for CJ. I didn't have the confidence of age and experience to be the mum that he needed me to be. He deserved better. After a week of an assessment that was meant to run for two, I was told I had failed; they had seen enough to determine that I couldn't give CJ adequate care. The shame and guilt of that has stained me forever.

Social Services asked for an independent psychological assessment to be done on me during the care proceedings. I had to go to York twice, to meet with the psychologist. Yet again, I was sent out of my comfort zone, completely alone, as I wasn't allowed anyone with me. I arrived at a big old building. Inside it looked like a museum, with dark green walls and ornate cream coloured coving with intricate designs, and dark hardwood floors. It was most certainly somewhere I'd never have come without being ordered to by Social Services. I got the impression that this would be an expensive place to visit. Feeling like this made me uncomfortable and took me out of the head space I needed to be in for this assessment to yield any positive results.

I may have outgrown my younger teenage self who compulsively lied to get her own way, but I hadn't escaped the consequences. The lies I had once told now followed me into this big old building and I was too scared, now that Social Services were involved, to come clean and face those lies. I was in a very foreign environment and lacked any kind of connection with the psychologist, which also worked against me feeling comfortable enough to be my true self. As such, I stuck with the lies I'd told years ago and felt obliged to play a role. I second-guessed what they wanted to hear and gave answers that either I thought would sound better, or that Jason had told me to say. And what Jason told me to say was consistent with what he had told Social Services.

I kept up a façade without realising I was painting a false and very sinister picture of myself. Ultimately, this backfired in ways I couldn't have possibly foreseen, and the report was damning. The psychologist identified me as having several mental health issues originating from the topics I'd lied about. This was when I realised what I'd done was wrong, and also that any attempt to correct these lies would come across as me trying to overturn the psychologist's assessment. I had to live with what she had committed to that report, knowing I'd done this to myself. In retrospect, I should have had the courage to tell the truth from the start, for my son, though I'm uncertain that this would have made a difference on the overall outcome. Ultimately, the failure of my care assessment and now the damaging and damning psychological report had sunk me.

Matthew was also given an assessment, but he took the incredibly brave decision to admit feeling unable to look after CJ alone, and he removed himself from the fight for sole custody. When we heard this, Jason wrongly assumed this would mean CJ would be returned to us, perhaps by some kind of default. Looking back, it's clear that Jason hadn't fully accepted the seriousness of our situation. Due to my failures, and Matthew letting CJ go, Social Services told me they would be filing for CJ to be removed from my care permanently and adopted. The drip-filled bath was now overflowing, and I had long since dropped beneath the surface. Nobody could save me, nobody knew how. There was no support from any services for the parent who gets left behind, and I felt that deeply.

Chapter Six

See You Soon

After the decision was made for CJ to be placed for adoption, the Court granted Social Services full custody, permanently stripping from me my parental rights. Contact was reduced over the period of a couple of months. Even though I had known that this was coming, by the time it arrived, the finality of it all and knowing there would be no miracle was all too heart breaking. Yet, when I was around other people I put on a face that told the world I was sad but managing fine. I never wanted my pain to be the cause of someone else's.

Before any goodbyes are said, Social Services ask you to take part in creating a life story book to go with the child. Though I never saw the finished product, I expect it was much like a 'this is your life' style book for your child up to the point of them being removed from your care permanently. For CJ's life story book, I sent some of my favourite photos of us together. I gave information about my likes and dislikes and about CJ's first few months with us. You can also write a letter to put in the book for when they are older, and my family were also able to write one. We wrote them very much under the impression that we may never see CJ again. It was the hardest letter I'd ever had to write.

As well as the life story work we were told that we would be given access to something called 'letterbox contact', which meant we could write one letter a year to him and could include a photo. Hopefully, we would then receive a reply from the adopters with a letter and a photo of CJ. There wouldn't be a back and forth, it would simply be one letter a year and any replies or comments would need to wait until the next year. We took the opportunity because it was better than having no contact at all. It was too painful to think that we would say goodbye and never hear from CJ again. I was willing to do anything to hold on to even a little part of him. I wasn't ready to let go.

Our first Christmas together was also our last. We didn't even properly celebrate. My favourite holiday of all time, one I had such grand plans for, passed by in the blink of an eye. We gave CJ gifts, but nothing too extravagant, and it felt odd to buy him anything that we wouldn't get to see him enjoy. I wish we had made more of an effort because I can't even remember the day, maybe it's one of the memories that are just too painful to recall. I do remember sharing CJ's first birthday with him and bringing in a miniature cake and a few balloons and decorations. Trying to decorate the Social Services contact room was like trying to put tinsel on a cactus, it might look pretty, but it still hurts. You can see in the photos that we took on that day that I have been crying; red faced and puffy eyes. I didn't get a single celebration with CJ to myself, to celebrate the way a mum should. Each day now was just bringing us closer to the last time we would see each other. I still wasn't ready.

April 18th, 2007. It was the day before my 19th birthday, and the day I had to say goodbye to my first-born son. Although, as Lisa repeatedly said, we weren't saying goodbye we were saying 'see you soon'. It was easier for my family to think like that. I couldn't. Hope had never done me any good thus far, it was easier to take this for what it was. A goodbye. We couldn't be sure if we would ever hear from or see CJ again.

I dressed smartly for the day, as if I needed to impress someone. I think I did it because I wanted to appear differently to how I felt inside. I believed I was a horrible

Mum, partner, ex-partner, and person for allowing all of this to happen. I thought it made me a bad person. I thought that all the social workers hated me, that they spoke about me behind my back (and not in the professional sense), and that they thought I was a child abuser. Not once did anyone tell me this, but my mind told me. I felt judged and detested by everyone, other than my family. Dressing older than my years, in grey pinstripe trousers and a cream shirt with my hair freshly washed and styled, made me feel less of the person I believed everyone thought me to be. But looking back, I also didn't feel like myself and I wish I had thought more about being comfortable than putting on an image that didn't reflect how I felt.

The final contact was in the same flat that my assessment had taken place in. As if it didn't hold enough bad memories, someone seemed to think the very place I failed my son for the last time, would be a good place to say a final goodbye, it felt like a cruel joke, and I was the punchline.

My Mum, Step-Dad, Lisa, her husband, Jason, and I all went and were met by two social workers. This time nobody took notes. There was no need to now. We gave CJ his lunch one last time, played with him, gave him some gifts as keepsakes and took our last photos together with him. At this point, saying goodbye was more for us than him. While he clearly still recognised me, and was content in my care, he had now been with his foster carer almost double the amount of time he was ever at home with me. His attachment to me was lost some time ago. Now, to him, I was just acting Mum. CJ's goodbye had been the day we left the hospital without him.

The social workers there that day were gracious enough to stay distanced and allow us to fully drink in our last few hours with CJ. One of the social workers had gotten to know us throughout the process and had always been kind and sympathised with us, and we were glad to have her there, although she too became emotional several times that day. Still, she offered support and comfort to my Mum, something for which I was so thankful.

During that final visit, we played with Ed the Duck, a puppet from mine and Lisa's childhood that CJ had taken a fancy to. As such, Ed was to go with CJ to his new home with his adoptive family. We watched as he ate his favourite snack, Quavers. As usual, he guzzled them down as he made silly faces in his highchair. It gave us all a good laugh, one we badly needed. As our time with CJ drew to a close, everyone said their own little 'See You Soon' and left to wait outside as he was passed to me to say my final goodbye. The social workers, still present in the room, pretended they couldn't hear, but it wasn't like there could be any privacy when I wasn't allowed to be left alone with him.

In a moment, that in equal measure both echoed and diverged from the first time CJ and I were ever alone together, I told him how much I loved him. I said that I would love him for the rest of my life and that there would never be a day where I wouldn't think of him. With tears filling in my eyes and drawing every ounce of mental strength I had to hold them at bay, I told CJ how sorry I was that I had failed to keep my promise to protect him, but that he would forever be my one and only. I sang 'You Are My Sunshine' to him, quietly, for one last time. Something I hadn't done since he was at home with me, and a single tear dropped from my eye onto his cheek. As I wiped it away, I kissed him softly on his forehead, breathed in his smell and I said goodbye. I passed him back to the social worker and I walked out to my family waiting in the car. Still holding back my tears.

I so deeply didn't want my final memories of CJ to be blurred by tears and that's not how I wanted him to see me, even though I knew he wouldn't remember it. This was made that much harder by every one of my family crying around me, but

I couldn't blame them. This was hard for everyone. The social workers walked to the cars with us, and my family all said another quick goodbye to each other as I sat in the back seat of Mum's car waiting to leave. I only had enough energy in me for one goodbye. It wasn't until we were on our way home that the damn burst and the sheer pain of my loss just flowed out of me like a river. I was in the depths of despair, sinking deeper by the second.

Chapter Seven
Grief and Change

I walked through the front door after our last contact and slumped onto the sofa. I felt numb. I just sat and cried; I didn't think I would ever stop. Using my sleeves to wipe my eyes every few minutes, my face was red and sore. Jason also cried and neither of us had the emotional energy to console the other. It was late in the afternoon when we returned and we didn't eat tea that evening, though this was normal for me those days. While much of CJ's things had gone with him, the cot remained. A now harrowing reminder that he was gone. He would never sleep in that cot again. I wanted to tear it down with my bare hands, but I wasn't that strong. I made a mental note to take it down the next day, along with anything else that reminded me of CJ. I had kept them for as long as possible, in the vain hope that the outcome would be favourable. Then, once we knew I had failed the assessments, I was reluctant to take it down because it felt like defeat. Now I couldn't pretend anymore and what was left was just a reminder that I was no longer a mum.

As Jason and me were putting things away the next day, I realised just how much CJ had taken with him. It was like we'd been slowly moving him out without even noticing. Bit by bit we sent more of his clothes and toys to him, and until then I hadn't quite noticed that there was barely anything left except for furniture. All that remained were trinkets of sentimental value. Apart from the furniture, everything else fitted into a box, not much bigger than a shoe box. That's all I had to show for five months of love and devotion, the only items left that proved I once had a son, and I was once a mother. Packing it all away felt like giving up that title. Somewhere among the trinkets lay the last pieces of my motherhood, useless, unused, and left with the memories to fade.

I spent the next few days in what I imagine hell would feel like. Devastatingly desperate to turn back the clock to a time before all of this happened. To see CJ, to hug him and kiss him and hold him as my own just one more time, knowing what lay ahead. I felt like I had taken what I had for granted. A week later, Mum and Lisa encouraged me to just go for a walk around the high street with them. I didn't want to be out in the world, I didn't want to see happy people and life carrying on as normal when it felt like mine had come to a complete stand still. I had gone from contact and court dates, assessments, and meetings with the solicitor to being left alone to wallow in heartache. Daily life had become so quiet, and empty and I wasn't ready to acknowledge that life outside of this flat still went on, but I did what they asked and reluctantly went along.

We knew now that we lived in the same town as the foster carer and we knew CJ was still with her, but we respected and understood the boundaries of what had happened, so we never even thought about going to see him, and we were lucky enough to have never seen them when we were out. Until that day.

Exactly a week after saying 'See You Soon', we were walking down a cobbled street and there was CJ and his foster carer right in front of us, with neither recognising the other until it was too late. In unison, Mum, Lisa, and I all gasped, and nobody was quite sure what to do or say. Lisa and Mum asked if they could say a quick hello. However, I felt like my heart had suddenly stopped beating. I spun around and turned my back to them, to quickly erase seeing them. I closed my eyes to try and stop the inevitable, but I couldn't, and the tears poured down my face.

It had taken so much mental preparation to survive our final meeting. I knew the day was coming, I had warning. But in that moment, on that cobbled street, I had none. I wasn't expecting to ever see him again, let alone just a week later. Saying goodbye to my son was the hardest thing I had ever had to do, and I couldn't do it all over again. Mum and Lisa said their hellos and when they finished they grabbed me, and we walked away. That was the last time I ever saw my baby CJ.

With all that had happened in such a short space of time, neither I nor Jason had been working and financially we had gotten ourselves into a mess. We were struggling to pay the rent and after a while we were asked to leave the property. About to be homeless, Jason' friend, Alex, very kindly allowed us to stay in his spare room. The eviction process had been happening in parallel to the court case for custody and I just didn't have it in me to even care, and so we never fought to keep the flat or even worried about the consequences until it was too late.

We packed most of our belongings into boxes and because we didn't know how long we'd be homeless, most of our possessions would be staying in boxes. We only packed into a suitcase the things we needed to easily access. This meant putting away CJ's things, knowing he would never need them again. I suddenly realised that I was leaving the only home I had ever brought him into, and it felt like another loss, one I hadn't considered until this point. I wasn't just saying goodbye to a flat, but to CJ's home with me. I was shutting away the memories, just like I was locking away my pain of losing him into the box in my mind, because most days it was too much to carry.

In some respects, once we'd moved, there was some comfort in not having a constant visual reminder of my time with CJ. No sensory souvenirs of a time too agonising to recall. For a while, my days were filled with a deep depression. I swung from too little or too much sleep but lack of a sense of purpose was constant. Jason and I stayed in the room at Alex's and watched TV. Jason was all I had now, and we were never apart, although living with a friend was sometimes helpful because it provided some social contact, and we weren't getting it from anywhere else. Most days, I just felt like I was treading water, weighed down by the waves of grief washing over me. Sometimes they were shallow, and I could still see the shore, other days I would drown, and the tears would flow. There was no aftercare from anywhere once CJ was adopted. I was aware of no services out there that could help and was left feeling alone in this. And if there was such a service, I lacked sufficient motivation to attempt to find it for myself. If I had lost a child to death, there were many places I could've gone for support. Losing a child to forced adoption is no less painful and it comes with extra dollops of shame and guilt. I can imagine no greater public shaming than forced adoption. Nobody I knew had ever experienced what I had, and I felt isolated. People around me could say kind words, platitudes mostly, although kindly meant ones. Nothing could help me, and I simply had to learn to ride the waves.

Writing seemed to help me a lot. I wrote out my feelings as if trying to expel the from my mind. I also wrote poems. This was the first one I ever wrote:

I never wanted you to go,

I only ever loved you so,

I tried my best to get you home,

But Mummy and Daddy came home alone.

You became my world when you were born,

And I promised to keep you safe and warm,

I promised you'd be my one and only,

I promised that I'd never leave you lonely.

I have kept my promises to this day,

Loving and missing you in every possible way,

Now I live with a piece of my soul that's gone,

You're in my thoughts and you help me stay strong.

Until the day you come looking I will sit, and I will wait,

I know this will happen, it's in our fate,

Please always remember that you hold my heart,

Until that love reunites us, and we're no longer apart.

We were at Alex's for a few weeks before we found a small one bedroomed flat to rent. It wasn't in my hometown, but it was in the same town that Jason' family lived, which he was elated about. I desperately didn't want to go, especially in a time when I still wanted to be close to my Mum and Lisa. We argued about the pros and cons of moving; I was scared to move far when neither of us drove, I also didn't know the town we were moving into, and I questioned if this were the right time to be moving somewhere that could make me feel even more separated from the world I knew. In the end Jason made me accept that finding a place to live while we didn't work was difficult, and landlords that would accept us were few and far between. We moved in almost immediately.

After settling in but still consumed by grief, Jason suggested having another baby. He was keen to be a Dad and firmly believed we'd be able to keep our baby, because he would be the biological Dad this time. He'd felt that Social Services would have no reason to get involved a second time, even though they made it clear that I would have to inform them if I ever got pregnant again. At the time, I had no idea how prevalent it is for someone who has lost a child to forced adoption to become pregnant again soon after. It seems like a pattern that many go through, and I was about to be one of those who plunged blindly into these statistics.

Chapter Eight
Meet the Parents

Within a couple of weeks of finding out I was pregnant, I started to become very sick and was in hospital on IV drips and close to needing a feeding tube. Hyperemesis gravidarum had returned once more. I was unable to get up out of bed for more than the few steps it took to get to the bathroom. I had stopped eating and was already losing weight. I was so weak that Jason had to help me into and out of the bath. Having told Social Services that we were pregnant again, we really hadn't heard much from them since our initial contact, at the point of our positive pregnancy test. We were in limbo as to what would happen next, and all we could do was wait. Naively we assumed no news, meant good news. Although we did hear from Social Services when I was six weeks pregnant, but not about the new baby, about CJ; more specifically, asking if I wanted to meet his adoptive parents, Peggy and Chris.

I never allowed myself, nor do I think I could have ever imagined the kind of couple who would end up being parents to my son. When it's not something you ever wanted to happen, it's almost impossible to then picture them with someone other than yourself. So, when I was asked, shortly before we said goodbye to CJ, what I wanted them to look for in adoptive parents, the question felt like a kick to the gut. To take my child and then to ask me to choose who to give him to, when all I truly wanted was for him to come home to me, seemed like cruel torture. Admittedly, I used to think that there could never be someone out there who would love my son the way that I did. Having never been in that position, I struggled to understand how anyone could bond with a child that isn't theirs in the same way I had bonded with my son. Even harder was the thought that he would grow to love someone else more than he loved me, though that time had long since passed.

Meeting his parents was a risk for me. If I didn't like these people in any way, I'd have spent my entire life being consumed by worry about a child that I no longer had the right to call my own. I was also terrified that I would meet the parents and they wouldn't like me. I didn't want them raising my son and hating me. I didn't know if this would affect how they felt about him and more than anything, I wanted him to know love. I wanted him to be loved, wanted, and adored. So, when Social Services asked me what to look for, I had said I wanted a couple with no other children and who couldn't have their own family. Although I know differently now, I was young and naive at the time and somehow felt that these conditions would mean the couple would love my son more. He would be more special to them somehow. I desperately wanted him to be for them, what he was to me. Wanted. Longed for. My one and only.

I had accepted the finality of the adoption. It had happened and I couldn't get my son back. I was meeting them for him now, I wasn't doing this for me. No matter how scared I was that they would hate me, worse that they wouldn't care enough to like me or hate me, as if all of it was pointless to them. It was important to me that they cared about meeting me, for his sake. I was told prior to the meeting that the couple was 'mature' for adopters which meant nothing to me, considering I wasn't exactly well versed in the statistics of the age of adopters. The meeting was held in the same room that most of mine and CJ's weekly contacts were held. Yet again, showing the unsympathetic nature of Social Services, who failed to recognise the harsh memories that this room would conjure for me. It was hard to go back there and certainly not where I would have chosen to meet CJ's adopters, but I had to push through that for CJ's sake.

I had no idea what to expect, after being given the impression that the couple were older than average adopters, but I was slightly relieved when I saw them, and they weren't the same age as my Grandad! In what could quite possibly have been one of the most awkward meetings of my life, I quickly felt at ease when I found them to be incredibly nice. We sat in the presence of a social worker, one I hadn't already met, and tried to get to know one another. Other than the basics of not asking questions about where they lived, we weren't briefed on what we could and couldn't ask or say to them, but I tried to be respectful and not get too emotional or speak badly about what had happened. I knew that the blame was not to be placed on the two people in this world who had come forward to love my son as much as I did. I won't pretend I remember a word of what was said, but I do remember the feeling I got from that meeting. I came away feeling like somehow, out of such a heart-breaking situation, my son was with two people that I honestly couldn't have hoped to be better.

Chapter Nine

Calm Before the Storm

Slowly but surely during this pregnancy, I started moving around. Provided I was steady and took things at a reasonable pace, then I was generally okay. I still couldn't eat or drink much, but I found I was less physically sick, though the nausea continued to be physically and mentally challenging. The sickness was a strain on mine and Jason' relationship, in the sense that we were no longer able to be as close as we once were. We went from being very co-dependent on each other after losing CJ, to being together but very separate once I started to become sick. Jason was a very physical person, that was his 'love language'. Whereas I am the type of person who has always found more love and passion from an emotional connection, Jason needed the physical and sexual side to feel happy.

Every time I stayed in hospital during the pregnancy, I came home and started to notice that he was more distant than usual. His focus had shifted from me onto spending time on the computer on his social media pages. On one occasion, I came home to find another woman's bracelet in our flat. His explanation was that he had found it and brought it home because he thought I would like it. To say I was suspicious was an understatement, so I asked him outright if he was cheating on me and he became angry at the insinuation. His fury scared me, as I had never seen him like that before, at least not when it was directed toward me. I took his outrage and emotional response to mean that he was genuinely insulted and therefore innocent, and I dropped the subject.

Jason' mum was a model who took part in photoshoots of various kinds, including glamour shoots. She was keen to get her family involved in her passion for photography and persuaded Jason and I to create a profile on an amateur modelling website. Part of me was flattered that anyone would think I looked good enough to be any kind of model, but for the most part I was doing this to get into Jason' mum's good books. I'm not sure why but we never got along; we never argued but I think she believed no girl was good enough for her son. Still, I always got the impression that I'd done something specifically to upset her, but as I had never said a bad word about her, it always confused me.

It was a side effect of being bullied that I was always in search of approval, especially from those who so outwardly seemed not to like me. If I felt disliked or hated by someone I was desperate to change their minds. So, when Jason said there was a photoshoot for me and it would be good for me to get out of the flat for a while, I said yes because I thought it would earn his mum's approval. Jason was thrilled about the idea of getting professional photos of me and deliberately looked for a glamour shoot, despite my being around four months pregnant.

He found a local Leeds photographer who wanted to have a shoot with me, and we set off for the day. I wasn't very well and feeling particularly nauseous, likely due to nerves. Jason had arranged the whole thing while I was unwell because he knew I was apprehensive about it but reassured me that all I had to do was show up. For the photoshoot, the photographer said he preferred partners not to be present as they can be distracting, so Alex came with us to Leeds and they both went to the pub while the photographer, Jack, collected me from the train station and took me to his studio.

We drove for about ten minutes to the outskirts of Leeds. It was unfamiliar territory, in a secluded area beyond the hustle and bustle of the city. We arrived at what looked like an abandoned factory or warehouse. The surrounding buildings looked much the same and I wondered whether we were doing the shoot 'on location' as a kind of urban-styled shoot, instead of in a studio. I'd have been hesitant from the outset if I didn't trust that Jason wouldn't have sent me to a photo shoot with someone who wasn't genuine, so I followed Jack as we walked through a small metal door to the side of the building.

Stepping inside it was pitch black and a chill ran through me as Jack slammed the door closed behind me, locking the bolts as he began making small talk. He flicked a switch on the wall and a sole dim lightbulb lit up further down the long narrow passage. Jack was surprised when I told him I hadn't modelled before, and I thought his reaction seemed a little over the top and likely his attempt at breaking the ice and boosting my confidence. We turned right at the end of the dark corridor and all around the black walls, along with everything in the building, seemed old and dusty. The place smelt damp and disused. Parts of the walls were coming away or missing completely to reveal plasterboard and pipes behind them. The space was divided into sections, but none seemed to have seen the light of day in long time. The building felt derelict but, as he used a key to get in, I assumed he had approved access. It was disorienting the way we turned a few times in several different directions, walked up a few flights of stairs and through some tight doorways, until finally arriving at Jack's studio. I wouldn't be able to find my way out alone.

There was an empty room with a chair that he said I could use as a changing room. It had a thin layer of carpet that was mostly worn away and discoloured. The room was cool but not too cold. He ran through some ideas with me for specific photos while looking through the items that he suggested I bring with me. I wasn't too sure what was in the suitcase until we both looked together because Jason had packed it. To warm up and get me used to being in front of the camera we did a few clothed shots first. I wore a cheerleader's style top and a mini skirt. It wasn't a pregnancy photoshoot, and I was the thinnest I had been since my pregnancy with CJ. You could barely tell I had a bump and to anyone who didn't know I was pregnant, it likely looked like your average stomach. I walked out of the 'changing room' and down the dark hallway, to the left there was no wall, but a plastic semi-sheer sheet had been hung up along the length of the wall. I found the opening and walked through to see his set up.

There were lights and back drops already out, with other material lying around to change the scenes as needed and a table full of props and cameras. Jack directed me to stand in the centre of the backdrop and began taking photos. He talked to me, making comments about how good I looked and cheeky remarks about my outfit that made me laugh and smile, again a likely tactic to boost my self-esteem. It worked. After the clothed shots, he asked me to change into some lingerie and he came and picked what he wanted me to wear. I was shaking, completely uncomfortable, but this felt like something I didn't have a choice in, especially once I was there. Jason was so excited for me to do this; I felt so much pressure to continue.

Walking back in with my hands awkwardly attempting to cover any modesty I had left, Jack walked over to me and looked me up and down. He ran his finger under the strap of my magenta bra as if he was adjusting it slightly. He again directed how he wanted me to sit, stand and lay in various positions. He brought down the lights for some shots when he asked me to remove my bra. I obliged, anxiously.

The photoshoot took an odd turn after these shots when Jack picked up a tiny bottle off the table and asked if I wanted any poppers. Not knowing what they were, and looking at the bottle, it seemed they could be drugs and I declined. I've never done anything like that in my life and I wasn't about to start now. He opened the bottle and inhaled it, heavily sniffing several times. He put it down and we returned to taking photos like nothing had happened. After about ten minutes Jack's demeanour changed. He was fidgeting more and seemed a little more hyperactive. I thought maybe he was just getting into the shoot and trying to lift the mood, as it was just the two of us alone. He asked me if I wanted to do some more risqué shots, suggesting tying me up for some bondage shots. Inside I was uneasy about it, particularly as it appeared he'd just taken some type of substance, but I agreed because I didn't know how he would react if I said no. It seemed easier to just go along to get along and get the photoshoot over and done with. I was aware that this was the first time I'd done anything like this, and this could quite possibly be very normal for modelling, maybe this was just how things were and it wasn't for me to say otherwise. I was in his world, not the other way around.

I was sat on the floor; my hands were now tied with tape to a pole above my head and my ankles were tied to another pole so I couldn't fully close my legs. I was blindfolded, which altered my senses. I became vividly aware of what I could hear and was more sensitive to the air around me. I was topless with tape around my breasts, but I had a small thong on that matched the bra I was wearing earlier. I could hear Jack clicking away with his camera, he was getting closer with each shot. Suddenly, I could feel his breath on my neck, he was directly in front of me. It almost felt like he was going to kiss me, but then I felt him move my underwear to the side and touch me. My body jumped out of shock, and I sternly said 'Stop!'. His reply was 'you want me to stop, you don't want me to touch you here?', and he touched me again, now knowingly against my wishes. My heart began beating like a horse bolting from the starting gate. I had the crystal clear and petrifying realisation, as if I hadn't noticed until now, that I was alone with a man I'd never met, who could have been anyone. We were in a seemingly abandoned building on the outskirts of town. I was now tied up in such a way that I couldn't physically stop him. All I had were my words. I raised my voice a little more and firmly said 'Stop it, now'. I sighed inwardly with relief when he did.

There was silence for a few seconds, and I braced for what I felt was an inevitable attack. I was terrified that this man could do anything he wanted to me, and not just to me but to my baby as well. As far as I knew, he wasn't aware that I was pregnant, and I didn't know if that would even matter to him. I heard him get up and walk away. After a minute or so I heard his footsteps coming toward me and I again braced myself to experience something horrible. Instead, he took off my blindfold and started untying me. He acted like he had just been joking and said he was trying to get me in the mood for the bondage style photos. It left me wondering if I'd blown it all way out of proportion.

We ended the photoshoot there but when I went to get dressed he followed me. As we walked into the room he closed the door and sat down on the chair. I went over to the other side of the room and gathered my clothes together. He asked me to come to him, but I refused and continued to get dressed. He asked me again, more impatiently and asked me to perform oral sex on him. I swiftly snapped 'No!' at him and zipped up my bag. 'I'm ready to go, NOW', I said with a strict tone. He turned and got up from the chair.

The walk through the pitch-black walkways to get out the building felt like a never-ending maze. Totally at his mercy and having to follow his every step, I was always ready to run in the opposite direction if he tried anything. My fight, flight reaction was dialled to maximum. As Jack opened the door and daylight blinded me, I felt like saying I would find my own way home, but I was still alone with him and defenceless if he turned at any moment. I got into his car and the closer we got to the train station the more I felt I could breathe again. We didn't say a word to each other on the journey. As he drove off, the reality of what had just happened hit me and I nearly collapsed in the street.

On arriving back at the flat, I slumped onto the sofa and burst into tears as I explained the terror of the ordeal to Jason. Yet he didn't seem angry and never asked if I or the baby were okay. Disturbingly, Jason almost seemed happy to hear the sordid details, like I was telling him a fascinating story. He didn't even seem surprised. That night when I was telling him what Jack had done, what I thought he was going to do to me and the baby, it was like I was telling Jason something he already knew about. When I asked if we should call the police, he said not to because he was worried that this would mean we wouldn't get the photos that Jack took, and it would have been for nothing. My heart sank that he seemed to care more about the photos than the dangerous situation he had placed me.

I had another photoshoot, non-glamour, booked the next day. I wanted to cancel it and never step foot near another photographer, but Jason encouraged me to 'get back on the horse', though this time he said he would insist on coming to the studio with me. I agreed, too lacking in energy not to. I sat in the empty bathtub that night with the shower raining down on me and I cried straight for at least twenty minutes. I didn't know if I was more shocked by what had happened, or by the fact that Jason seemed to care so little about it, and more about the photos. The next day we went to the photoshoot, and I was unwell plus what had happened less than 24 hours earlier had taken its toll on me. I was petrified of what to expect that day. Jason did stay with me the whole time and the shoot went off without a hitch. The photographer was an older gentleman and was very nice. Still, I was feeling worse by the minute, and I could tell that my hyperemesis was returning and that I needed to be in the hospital. Once admitted, I was glad to be alone for a few days. I desperately wanted to tell someone what I'd gone through, but I took a few days to get better, and I kept quiet because I knew Jason wanted the photos so badly, it was the only time I've ever been thankful to be in the hospital and the for the first time in a while I felt calm.

Chapter Ten

My Abuser

When I returned home mid-week from hospital, Jason asked if Alex could visit that weekend. He was an avid photographer who knew a bit about photography and Jason wanted to get some photos of us together so we could have one printed onto canvas and displayed on a wall. I was happy for Alex to do that for us, and it allowed him to get a bit of experience too. Over the next few days, Jason suggested to me that I should let Alex take photos of me in a glamour modelling style to help me get back into it again. I said no at first, but after Jason' persistent questioning about it I grew tired and said yes. While in the hospital I'd decided not to carry on modelling, but I hadn't found the courage to tell Jason. Now didn't feel like the right time.

Alex came around on the Saturday and Jason and I dressed in our best clothes, and we headed outside to get some nice photos together. Then we shared a good evening watching a film and the boys had a beer together before we started with the glamour style photos. After a few alone, Jason said he wanted to do some photos with me, which made me feel slightly less awkward, so I welcomed this at first, until he started to take my bra off in front of Alex without asking me. Although I went along with it, my mind ran back to the first photoshoot and the feeling of needing to go along to get along.

The pressure of feeling like I couldn't say no because it reminded me of being back there. It was easier, just like before, to keep Jason happy. Jason started to kiss me and touch me, and Alex kept taking photos. During a short break, Jason asked me if I wanted to let Alex join in. I couldn't remember his exact words but was shocked at what he was asking of me, especially so soon after the horror of my first photoshoot. Regardless of whether I was well, or pregnant, this just wasn't something I had ever expressed any need or desire for, and I was perplexed at where this side of Jason had come from. Since our lack of physical intimacy from the beginning of our pregnancy it was like he was going in to overdrive sexually and I didn't like this side to him. This was no longer the kind, attentive and caring man I'd met once upon a time. I asked to stop taking the photos and I went to bed. I felt sick to my stomach, and not just because of the hyperemesis.

I was utterly exhausted from the stress, and I still wasn't over it from the week before. I closed my eyes and heard the door open in front of me. Our room wasn't big, but it wasn't a box room either. There was just enough space to have one chest of drawers against the wall at the bottom of the bed to the right of me, and a double bed that faced the window. The door was about a metre from me, and I slept on the right side of the bed. Jason got undressed and climbed into bed without a word. The light in the bedroom was still on. I always wore a top to bed and just my underwear on the bottom. Jason usually slept in his underpants. I felt him move closer to me and I could tell he was naked. He brought his left arm over the top of me and touched my breast through my top; a move I recognised as him indicating that he wanted to have sex. We hadn't had sex since the time we got pregnant, partly because I was sick and unable to, and partly because with everything that had happened of late I hadn't felt up to it. I softly took his hand off me and said sorry, but I wasn't in the mood. Sex was the last thing on my mind. After a few minutes, Jason moved even closer to me, shaping his body around mine. He again moved his left arm over me and around my mid-section. I felt his right arm slide under my head and around my front, pulling me into him and resting his hand on my chest. My first thought was that he wanted to snuggle. It was uncomfortable to lay like that, so I tried to nudge him away, but he didn't move. With his left hand, he moved slowly downward and then moved my underwear to the side. As he did this he put his right hand over my mouth. I froze.

Jason pulled me even further back until I couldn't go back anymore. He forced himself into me and he raped me. I was a mess of confusion, hurt and betrayal. I didn't understand why he was doing this to me, why sex meant so much to him that he needed to take it from me. He was hurting me; this wasn't something he had done before. Inwardly I was screaming, yet only a whimper leaked out from the pain coursing through me. Through my tears, I was staring at the white door in front of me and the magnolia walls that felt like they were boxing me in. I could imagine Alex on the other side of the door, laying on the sofa. I was in two minds. One that desperately wanted him to hear me crying for help and to come in and stop Jason. The other, not wanting him to come in and witness this, maybe through embarrassment or shame. When it was over Jason got up and went to the bathroom. I lay there, trying not to throw up, shaking and unsure if what just happened was what I thought it was. He was no longer my knight in shining armour, that title was long gone, now he was my abuser.

Chapter Eleven

RJ

After the night Jason attacked me, he acted like nothing had happened. It became clear that he either didn't see what he had done as rape, he didn't understand that it was, or he just didn't care. I didn't know which scared me more. I found the courage to ask him what, in his mind, had happened, but he shrugged it off as though it was nothing. His response did not help my understanding of how he saw it. Realising I needed to be more specific, I asked him why he kept going when I was crying for him to stop, and why he put his hand over my mouth. It came out like an interrogation, but I knew if I didn't get it out I would get to a point where I was too scared to keep on going. In response, Jason simply said that he thought I was okay with it, that I wanted it because I made no physical effort to stop him, and the crying was due to the pain.

Taking a second to think about what he had said, I partially wondered if I had gotten things very wrong. Did I not do enough to make it clear to him that I didn't want to have sex? Was my freezing the reason I saw it as rape, and he didn't? I said I wasn't up for it, I nudged him away but not with great force. I was tired and perhaps I didn't make it obvious enough. Maybe I should have screamed. I began to doubt myself. I didn't push the matter further because I started to think that I was to blame for what had happened. I never brought up that night again, feeling guilty for thinking so badly of him and mislabelling sex as rape, and I dismissed how I felt about it. Life went back to how it was before; I was sick again with the hyperemesis and started being readmitted to hospital regularly. We lived in a different district now and didn't know any of the social workers, so after a brief meeting with Social Services to introduce themselves to us, they told us they would do an assessment once the baby arrived, although we could expect to hear from them again before then.

We found out we were having a baby boy and were so excited, yet the news triggered something inside of me. As the pregnancy progressed, I was beginning to picture what the baby would look like, and every time I did this I could only picture the baby looking like CJ. While the tide of grief felt like it had gone out a little, I was merely distracted by the other issues going on, and now the tide was coming back in, and I was thinking about CJ a lot of late. I was wondering what he was doing and remembering the time I had with him. When I was trying to think of names for the new baby, my brain thought it was a great idea to call him CJ, and it would be like I had him back again. This was when I realised that I wasn't keeping my head above water with my grief nearly as much as I thought I had been. I decided it was best to keep this momentary lapse of judgement to myself and we would choose a different name for this very different child. But I knew then that when I agreed to have a baby with Jason, I hadn't truly wanted another baby, I was wanting the one I already had.

I never made it past being out of hospital for more than a few days at a time after this. When the social worker did eventually visit, it was to explain what was going to happen, she had to come to the hospital to see me. I was thankful I had my own room, though it still felt awfully invasive to have a social worker visit me in hospital. It wasn't the best of times to be discussing such a sensitive subject. She told me that they were unable to do the assessments before the baby was born and therefore it was likely that our son would not be allowed to come home with us and would go straight into foster care. Contact would be set up much like it was with CJ, once a day during the working week only. I want to say that I was upset, and I was, but nowhere close to what it felt like when it happened with CJ. Despite how positive Jason was, I don't think I ever truly let myself believe that we would get away with not having Social Services involved and being allowed to bring our baby home without question.

On November 30th, 2007, I started to get twinges while I was in the hospital. I unexpectedly had a show, where the mucous plug comes out of the cervix, and it was decided that I should have the steroid injections to help develop baby's lungs in case I went into premature labour, especially as CJ arrived early. You have the first injection, then another 24 hours later. I was absolutely terrified of needles and I'm not ashamed to admit that I asked Mum to come and hold my hand. The injection itself wasn't that bad, but the stinging after pain was terrible, though it passed relatively quickly. I was told prior to the jab to tell Mum to bring in something cold to hold against it afterwards as it can help. You'd have thought she would bring an ice pack, maybe a bag of peas. Oh no, she brought a pint of milk for me to lay there and hold against my buttock waiting for the pain to pass. It gave me a laugh at least. The doctors decided if labour was to start they wouldn't try to stop it and after 24 hours without signs of labour I was given the second steroid injection.

The next day I noticed I started to get twinges again. Little pains that I recognised right away. I told the nurses I thought contractions were starting and I phoned Mum and Lisa to come in. With having a private room this time, they could come in even outside of visiting hours. Things happened quickly last time, so I didn't want to risk waiting. When they came we just sat and chatted away. I was laughing hysterically through the first few hours before I was in established labour, which is when you are three to four centimetres dilated. Around half three in the afternoon, I couldn't keep still, and I knew things were moving along quite quickly. We were rushed down to the labour ward when they realised I was already dilated about five centimetres.

The room was a hub of activity with many people dashing in and out of the room, far more than I was comfortable with but I didn't have much choice. Machines were brought in and nobody was talking to me. It was extremely overwhelming. At 4:50pm, after only an hour and twenty minutes of active labour, our little boy, who we named RJ, entered the world ten weeks early. I didn't get to hold him, and I only saw him for the briefest of seconds. He wasn't crying the way a full-term baby would and swarmed over by a team of doctors checking him over, while the nurses tended to me. RJ was promptly taken up to the neo-natal intensive care unit (NICU).

After my last birth, as soon as CJ was born everything calmed down, but that didn't happen this time. Half of the medical staff had left with RJ, yet there were still a lot gathering around me. It took me a while to realise the fuss still going on in the room was directed at me. I was losing a lot of blood and they were growing concerned because my heart rate was high too. I was told I may need a blood transfusion, and this scared me, and all the rushing around was scaring me so much that I requested them to just leave me be for five minutes and see what happened. I felt confident that if they stopped talking about things that were causing me a lot of anxiety and just left me to calm down, that I would improve. I could barely take anything in with all the noise and people around me; it was all too much. I'd just given birth and hardly seen my son, and I wasn't thinking about myself.

The bleeding slowed and they agreed to leave me. It was just myself, Jason, Mum and Lisa in the room. I asked for the TV to be turned on so I could focus on something other than RJ. We all sat and chatted about the birth with Top Gear on the TV in the background, and after a while my heart rate came down and the bleeding plateaued. I was shaky and weak for some time, though once I had eaten I felt much better.

With no baby to hold and no medical staff in the room now, it seemed surreal that I had just given birth. It looked more like a horror movie scene with blood-soaked sheets and equipment left lying around. Not having that first hold with RJ stalled my emotions. I felt empty. Then it hit me, RJ looked nothing like CJ did when he was born. They were, of course, two completely different babies. I didn't get the rush of love; I didn't feel happy for having had another baby. I just felt a painful reminder that this baby wasn't CJ.

Chapter Twelve
The NICU

A couple of hours after giving birth, the nurses gave us permission to visit the Neonatal Intensive Care Unit (NICU) to see RJ. I was wheeled up in a chair as I was still very weak from all the blood loss. It was dark and hot in the NICU and there was a song of machines beeping all around us, yet somehow it was quiet, and the low lights gave a sense of calm and comfort. RJ was in the bottom room at the end of the corridor. My first real glimpse of him was in a tiny Perspex house. He was connected to various machines with a jungle of wires coming from him. He wore a mask over his face that was assisting with his breathing. I imagine it's a hard job for such a tiny baby out in the world ten weeks before they're meant to be here.

RJ weighed only 2lbs 13ozs, and I'd never seen a baby so small. It was incredibly surreal and because he wasn't moving or crying, it was displacing to be there and see him like that. I was still in some degree of shock and it was overwhelming. I slipped my hand in to the incubator through a small port hole window on the side and placed my finger on his hand, which wasn't much bigger than my fingernail. In all transparency, I felt nothing. I feigned what I imagined I should show, seemingly quite well as nobody noticed, but I was far too aware that this little one, while beautiful in his own right, was not the baby I wanted to be with right now.

Jason was reluctant to leave but as we were local, and RJ was stable, the parents' rooms in the NICU were best reserved for those who didn't live close by and whose babies were much sicker. I returned to the maternity ward to get a few hours rest and could visit to see RJ whenever I wanted.

As the sun rose the next day, Jason and I were at the unit with RJ sitting by his incubator and just watching as the world passed him by. The NICU is exceedingly warm and, even though it was the beginning of winter, we were sweating. On the unit the rooms work a little like classes. Each baby will start their journey in a specific room depending on their gestation, size, and health. As they grow, improve and develop, they move across to a different room, each time getting closer to the entrance to the ward and quite literally closer to home. RJ started in the very first room, furthest from the door. He had a very long way to go, but he was a little soldier.

After some sleep, I could see RJ with fresh eyes. Although, looking back, I know I didn't bond with him in the way I should have. I was happier to see him after a night's rest. Looking at him, he felt familiar, and he was perfect and so small, and I smiled when I saw and touched him, but there was always this harrowing grief that he wasn't CJ. I couldn't find a way to let him in to my heart, I wanted to so badly, but I also think a part of me was trying to shield myself from any further pain and loss. If I loved RJ the way I did with CJ, I was scared it would hurt that much more if things didn't work out. And I wasn't sure I could face that all over again.

Over the course of the next few days, our families came to meet RJ and dote on him as much as you can when you're unable to hold a baby and you're in a very foreign and sterile environment. On the third day of RJ being in the NICU, I was finally able to hold him. I had wondered if this may be the trigger that flipped the switch in me that would turn on my feelings for him, but they never came. I cried and people assumed it was for RJ. I let them. When it came time for me to leave the hospital, I know I should have felt bad leaving RJ there alone, but it felt like a

76

relief to get away from the maternity unit where all I would see were other mums getting the experience I wasn't getting. Not only were their babies' full term and in their arms, but they were happy and overjoyed. It was yet another constant reminder of a past too painful to awaken in my mind.

After RJ was born, we knew we'd need to move to a new house with room for him to come home to, should that happen. I was excited thinking this meant we could look to move back to Skipton, but Jason said he didn't want to move there, and he wanted to stay close to his family. His family having also recently relocated to a different town, we ended up finding a house there and I was even further from my family. It was a town I didn't feel comfortable moving to, but a time where I could be honest about my own feelings, a time when they even mattered, had long since passed. We'd moved mid-December, so we were in the new house for Christmas.

Christmas and New Year passed in a blur. We all went to see RJ on Christmas morning then as was tradition, we went to Mum's house for Christmas dinner. We chose not to celebrate the New Year at all because we had no idea what to expect for the coming year. Starting with more of the same, we were hoping it would end differently. Jason was still so adamant that RJ would come home when they saw that we were good parents. He wouldn't even contemplate what would happen if we didn't get custody of RJ.

Having a baby in NICU is hard. We were lucky that RJ was never that sick. He just needed time to get big and strong. We went to sit with him every day for most of the day and evening, only returning home once the sun had gone down. We just sat and watched, keeping him company, and letting him know his mum and dad were there with him. The days all resembled each other, and they soon turned into weeks. RJ was doing so well, and it was looking like it may soon be time for him to come home. Except he wouldn't be. Since Social Services still hadn't completed an assessment, RJ had to go to a foster home when he left the hospital. Our fight to keep him had only just begun and, much like when I brought CJ into the hospital, the day RJ went home we had to say goodbye to him there and leave before a stranger came to take him to his foster placement. We didn't get the going home advice on how to look after him, nobody congratulated us or asked if we were excited, because they all knew he wasn't coming home with us. Even though we said goodbye, it never truly felt like I had said hello.

Chapter Thirteen
The Wedding

We came home from the hospital to, yet another empty nursery and I cried. I was bewildered as to why I was so upset when I knew I hadn't yet bonded with RJ, even though I knew I did love him in my own way. I figured it was a mixture of memories, hormones, and the fact that despite there being no bond I was still all too aware that a part of me, a little person with my blood running through them, was out there without me and that was heart breaking.

Daily contact during the week had been arranged and would start on the Monday at a local community centre. This was a much nicer venue than the Social Services office. We had access to a kitchen and there were comfortable seats in the rooms, and there were even a few sensory toys available. This allowed us to make the most of our daily few hours with RJ. In an environment geared more towards children, we were fully able to display most of our capabilities as parents. A social worker sat with us each day and as we were in a new area and didn't know them, they took the opportunity to talk to us and get to know us during our contact sessions, which created a much better atmosphere and relationship.

On the outside of the daily contact, we were fighting for our right to have an assessment. Both Jason and I needed representation and were to be assessed both jointly and separately because we weren't married. Amongst all this we hadn't thought about marriage much. Jason had proposed in the middle of the court case for CJ. He'd made a big song and dance about it at a local restaurant in front of my family and I said yes, but we hadn't much discussed it since then. I didn't think it was the right time for him to propose and he probably thought that I needed some good news, but it just felt like the wrong time for a celebration. No sooner had we got engaged than we quietly put on the back burner because it wasn't a priority. However now RJ was here, we planned on getting married, though admittedly after all that had happened when I was pregnant, I would have been happy to hold off.

At home, things weren't going well within our relationship. We had started to plan the wedding, which we arranged for my birthday that year. Jason was excited and I was good at faking a smile as I went along with all the planning. We didn't want anything big, nor could we have afforded it. A church wedding in the town we just moved from, even though we weren't religious, and a small reception at a local venue, was about all we could pull together. Tensions at home were high because the more we talked about it, and the more Social Services delved into our lives to gather information for their files, the harder it became to wear my faux smile.

I knew I couldn't continue to carry on like this, so I planned to sit down with Jason and tell him that I just wasn't up to getting married while everything was going on with RJ. I thought that if I cooled everything down slowly then it would be easier, so rather than breaking everything off completely, I was hoping that telling him I just wanted to postpone would be easier for him to handle. I sat down on my desk chair in the bedroom as he was stood across the room at the other side of the bed. At the last second, with my heart in my mouth, I realised I had to be fully honest, and I told him that I had been having second thoughts about our relationship and I couldn't marry him.

He was immediately angry; a reaction I hadn't expected. I thought he'd be more hurt and upset. As he raised his voice, I did so too in response to his yelling. In a back and forth of 'I can't do this' and 'you can't leave me', out of nowhere Jason jumped over the bed and lashed out, hitting me across the side of my head. I let out a single scream as the pain shot through my ear. I clutched the side of my head and cowered, not knowing if further blows were coming. I couldn't speak for a few minutes and I sat there shaking and crying. After initially going back across the room, Jason rushed back over to me, and I flinched thinking he was about to hit me again. He got down on his knees and explained how sorry he was, and he just lost control and so desperately didn't want me to leave. He started to cry and begged me not to go, claiming he'd never do it again and he would do better. Still stunned, I took a deep breath and I said I would stay. Now too scared to leave. After that night Jason rarely left me alone. I couldn't leave the house alone and he would invite himself along to every outing I went on.

Once RJ was born, I'd tried to get back in touch with friends from school and I was regularly going out with them, which was giving me a little bit of myself back each time, and one friend, Lena, was quickly becoming my best friend. We went shopping, we had nights out, or even nights in. Unfortunately, none of these nights were without Jason unless it was a girl's night, such as my hens' night. I knew the girls weren't too keen on him, but they put up with him for me. I was so glad of that because it made my life that bit easier. At some stage, before the big day, almost every one of my family and friends had asked me if I was happy. Although I told them I was, to keep up appearances, it was clear my mask was slipping, and I needed to work harder if I was going to fool Social Services for twelve weeks under close supervision and constant surveillance.

The day after Jason had hit me, I managed to get a few moments alone with the social worker during contact, when Jason went to make RJ's bottle. Luckily, I had no visible marks to explain away. I'd been worried that if I left Jason, my chances of getting custody of RJ would be all but gone. Despite still not feeling a bond, I knew he was mine and I felt a strong urge to fight for him, although I suspected that was more to do with losing CJ, than keeping RJ. Still, I wanted to know. I needed to know. I asked her if I wanted to do this alone, what would happen. She told me in no uncertain terms that it would be much better if we were married because it would show we were in a stable relationship and we were committed to one another. My heart sank in that moment. I knew that meant that without Jason, I would lose RJ. I resigned myself to the fact that I no longer had any choice. I had to marry Jason.

A week before the wedding, at the beginning of April, we were given a court date for the final decision on whether Jason and I would be granted a place at a live-in assessment centre. We had been fighting for months to be given this chance to prove ourselves as suitable parents and the judge finally granted it, and the assessment was arranged to start in June. With that, on the 19th of April 2008, my 20th birthday, the wedding went ahead. Jason' mum disliked me so much that, for reasons still unknown to me, she didn't come to the wedding. On the day, as Lisa was tying up the back of my dress, and we were about to leave for the church, she told me that if I wanted we could both jump in her car and drive away, I need only say. I paused. As sure as I am that my eyes probably told her that I wanted very much to take her up on the offer, I wasn't ready to give up on RJ. So, I said was fine, I was happy, and that I wanted to do this. That was my last chance to back out.

Social Services let RJ briefly attend the ceremony with a social worker and we got a few photos of with him. He was dressed in a little pink waistcoat we'd bought him and looked adorable. It was the first time many of our family had seen him, but only Jason and I were permitted to hold him, which was embarrassing, but at the same time I was grateful that they allowed it because it would have been easier for them to deny our request to have him there.

The day went smoothly, the church ceremony I'm sure seemed lovely, and afterwards we took photos with our family but being a cold day most of them left to go up the road to the reception venue. Set up in a room above a local bar we had decorated the room with pink and silver 'Just Married' banners and put white tablecloths down and we had a candle in the centre of each table. There was a buffet followed by dancing and karaoke. It wasn't a formal event, there were no speeches or set menus. The party went on until late into the night and then we went to a hotel for our wedding night. I was so exhausted that consummating the marriage was the last thing on my mind, something I think Jason didn't approve of, but he didn't argue with it either. We lay on the bed opening our cards and the few gifts we got as most of our family gifted us money. We sat on the bed and talked about the day, and I fell asleep before I even took off my dress. While I know the basics of the day, rather thankfully I don't remember much of the details anymore and I'm okay with that.

Chapter Fourteen
Trapped

A month after the wedding we used the money that family gave as gifts to go on a honeymoon to Spain. Part of me was scared about going abroad with Jason, but I also thought a little away time might be good. I'd spent the last month since the wedding telling myself that Jason would never hurt me again, that he seemed genuinely sorry when he'd hit me and maybe it changed something in him. Though I didn't want to marry him, this was my best shot at getting RJ home and, if we were successful, I wanted that home to be as happy as possible. I had to try, and I hoped that this holiday would be a new beginning and would wash away all the misery of the past year. I longed to feel safe and loved again. It wasn't overly hot while we were there, not yet in the high season of the key summer months. We spent time at the nearby beach, went swimming in the hotel pool and explored the local town of Torremolinos. I'd been here before with my family when I was 15 years old. It was my first ever holiday abroad and seemed so long ago now. Jason and I stayed at the same hotel this trip, so I was somewhere familiar and could find my way around, which made me feel slightly more at ease.

Returning from the honeymoon, Jason wanted to get the house ready for RJ before we left for our assessment. He fully expected that RJ would be coming home with us. We rebuilt CJ's cot and his chest of drawers. The room was a pale-yellow colour with a beige carpet and a built-in closet, which was great for much needed storage space for other items such as a baby bath. We placed a few toys out in the room that we purchased when RJ was born, or things he was gifted for his first Christmas.

Getting into the homely mood, we also decorated our room in a very dark blue, almost navy colour so it would feel fresh on our return home. The room was large, so it didn't look too overpowering, and we managed to find some navy and gold silk bedding to match the room which made it feel luxurious. I struggled to envision RJ coming home and getting the house prepared was simply going through the motions in my mind. Jason' excitement did sometimes carry me off into a land of hope, but it was always very brief and the fall back to reality was harder each time. I wouldn't allow myself to get too far ahead of the situation, something in me just didn't feel right.

One night, shortly before we were due to move to the assessment house I awoke in the night with Jason on top of me. He'd been having sex with me as I slept. Still half asleep, and confused I told him to stop, and he did. At first I wondered if I was having a nightmare, after last year, it wouldn't have been the first time but then I noticed the brisk coldness in the room, and the contrast of the warmth of the sheets on my skin. This was real, I was awake. Panicked and a little scared, and because he'd done as I asked, I decided it would be best to close my eyes and attempt to go back to sleep and not tackle the issue right now. I couldn't help but wonder if he'd done this before and I hadn't woken up. Surely I would have? Then the self-doubt started. Had I done something to make him do this? Or was I sleep talking and he thought I was awake? We hadn't had sex since I was pregnant with RJ, since 'that' night when he didn't stop despite me crying. I know for Jason it's an important part of a relationship, but it just wasn't something I wanted to do with him anymore. I had so many questions swirling round in my head. Did he want me to know he was doing it, was it a punishment for trying to leave him before we got married. Maybe he just wasn't able to control himself? I laid there with my eyes closed, but my mind awake with worry until I felt him moving closer to me. I was too scared to react, I didn't want to talk, I certainly didn't want to sex with him, and so I pretended to be asleep.

I felt the air move past me as his arm reached over me, followed by his body as he climbed on top me. I remained frozen in fear. He pulled my underwear to the side, lowered himself into me and started to have sex with me, believing that I was asleep. It felt easier to let him presume that was the case, rather than risk him hurting me if I tried to stop him. Around ten minutes later he finished, gently lifting himself off me and standing up. He tiptoed to the bathroom trying to stay quiet so as not to wake me, still none the wiser that I was already awake. He came back moments later and went to sleep as if nothing happened. For the lasting hours of the night, I lay in the quiet darkness. Though I now had my eyes open, there was no light in the room and my eyes could only adjust so much to see a vague outline of the furniture in the room. Memories came flooding back, images I wished I'd forgotten but I hadn't; scrolling along my brain like a slideshow I couldn't turn off. As the sun came up and I wiped away the last teardrops of the night, I got up and went downstairs to sit in solace until Jason woke up and I had to wear a smile again.

When Jason awoke about an hour later and came downstairs, I didn't know how to approach what happened. Jason didn't even know I was awake, and I was so scared he'd get angry and wouldn't be able to reign it in. I had to say something though, I'd woken up and asked him to stop at one point, so I knew that was a way to start the conversation. Asking Jason why I woke up with him on top of me, he played it off like he assumed I was awake and that he'd only just started and wanted to see if I wanted it. Making it as clear as I could, I told him not to do anything unless he had confirmation that I was awake, such as me responding to him vocally. He seemed annoyed that I was telling him not to do it, raising his voice slightly and asking how he was meant to know when I want it, because I never ask for it anymore. I apologised, my heart starting to beat a little faster with his temper showing. I dared not push it any further, so I left it there. I sincerely hoped that there had been some major misunderstanding and that telling him not to do it once I had gone to bed, would clear that up and there would be no repeat of this.

But that was not the last time that I woke up to find Jason having sex with me and I'd become too afraid to say anything, to push him off or fight him in any way. Too frightened of the person I now knew him to be, and the consequences of such, so I continued to imitate being asleep, feeling like it was not only the safest but my only option. This became an almost daily occurrence. In my waking life I had to pretend that I didn't know. There were days I would wake up with my underwear wet or broken and still I had to feign ignorance, which came in the form of me just keeping my mouth shut. He never said a word, and I was too scared to. There were days I wanted my life to be over, times that I wanted to run far away because it all felt like too much. Yet, when I saw RJ, and in front of Social Services I had to act like we were the picture perfect, loved up newlyweds. It was the only chance I had of bringing my son home. I wasn't going to give up trying.

Chapter Fifteen
Ready

In the few weeks before we went to the assessment house we were told by social workers that they felt confident we had nothing to worry about. Having seen us almost daily for several hours in contact, and getting to know us, they felt we would do well and had no concerns at all. This gave Jason so much hope that he thought it was a done deal and that RJ would come home with us. I still had my reservations, though I wondered now if my feelings, or lack thereof, were clouding my judgement. I wondered whether I just lacked the ability to hope anymore because I certainly didn't feel like I had a lot to be positive about at home.

The week before we left we had to start visiting the foster carer's house to wake up RJ, then we would take him to the usual contact centre, and we'd come back with him in the early evening to put him to bed. Effectively, we were taking over much of his day-to-day care in preparation for us spending 24 hours a day with him, seven days a week. It was hoped that it would strengthen the bond a little with RJ, who still didn't know us properly. It was uncomfortable to be in someone else's house again, but not being alone and having Jason there did help this time around. The days were long and not being in a proper house was difficult, but we made it work and having such a positive relationship with our social worker helped as she would always jump in with helpful tips and suggestions if we needed them. We could use the toys from the playgroup area in the building and we could go out into the back garden for air, which was greatly appreciated given it was July and quite stuffy to be in the one room all day.

The time came for us to go to the assessment, which was to take place at Cheshire House. Our social worker drove us there and stayed until we were settled in. The house was a large, Victorian style red brick building that had been converted into a few self-contained flats with a communal area downstairs for a playroom. There were also a few offices for the staff, and the garden was communal too. We stayed in the flat on the very top floor and the door to our flat opened directly into the small living area, decorated in a neutral cream colour. There was a sofa to the left against the back wall and a cot along the wall across from this for RJ to sleep in. He had to sleep here as there were cameras in this room so they could always monitor us; they could also always hear us in this room too. The kitchen was to the far left of the room and it was small but with plenty of storage, and all the amenities we needed. There was a window to the right of the front door that overlooked the back garden, and the bedroom was right next to this. To the left of the bed was the bathroom, an en suite with a toilet, sink and a bath. As this was the only bathroom we had to call a staff member to be with us when we bathed RJ, otherwise we had to keep RJ in the living room unless someone was with us. They couldn't see us in our bedroom, but they could hear us in there. If you are accepted to go to Cheshire House, it would only be if it were deemed safe enough for you to stay in a room alone with your child, while being constantly monitored.

We could bring some home comforts to make the flat homely, such as throws and bedding, and even some photos because although the flat was nicely decorated, it was basic, like a bed and breakfast. We were shown around and told how everything worked and then we were left to settle in with RJ. It was surreal to suddenly have him with us, in a space that wasn't our own. Knowing we were being watched and listened to, made life a lot harder. Even when you knew you weren't doing anything wrong, being observed made us hyper-aware of our every action. I was already supressing so much of how I felt, I didn't know how much I was going to be able to hide here but at least I knew I was safe; I could breathe easier knowing Jason won't do anything while they could see and hear us.

On our first full day, one of the on-site social workers explained the plan they had for us and outlined what they expected to see from us. The plan included goals to achieve and listed specific things they would be looking out for. It detailed a daily, step by step, activity and meal plan that we had to follow for RJ, and they worked with us around household budgeting, also planning a timetable to go shopping at the local supermarket and everything we would do with RJ during the day. Until RJ went to sleep at night, every part of our day was mapped out. It was full on and very demanding compared to what we had been used to. When preparing meals and bottles, the social worker would come to watch as we did it to see if this were being done correctly. During this assessment, there was a difference though, if there was something I didn't know how to do or I was unsure of in any way, I would be offered help. I appreciated this so much, but it did feel somewhat like having a teacher with you who was constantly grading your every move. It was exhausting. If you were out of the living area too long when there was nobody in the flat with you, they would come over the intercom and ask if we were okay. The only time they didn't do this was at night.

One of the things on our impeccably planned weekly itinerary was for me to attend a local mother and baby group. I wasn't asked if I wanted to do this, it was something they expected me to do as part of RJ's care at home, and so I had to do it there to show that I would willingly take part. I had to go with the social worker, who had to then explain who she was for safety reasons and this immediately made me feel completely out of place. Other than my four friends at home, I wasn't a sociable person. I was at this point, performing for a large proportion of the day and attending a group where I had to mix with other mums with seemingly perfect lives, and babies who went home with them without being watched, and who were dressed better than me, and likely weren't hiding an abusive relationship, was no easy task for me. I was in hell. I was so completely out of my comfort zone, way, way out of it. The comfort zone wasn't even on this map of the perfect lifestyle they had us emulating, and it was taking all I had not to break down. I was doing all this for RJ, I had a sense of duty to him. Jason had personal time with RJ in the playroom at Cheshire House, but nothing quite as public as mine because they assumed that Jason would eventually find a job and not be home during the day. This felt like an unfair advantage, in that they were paying more attention to my duties, and it began to feel like they liked Jason and approved of him and were targeting me. I was always the one who had to do the bottles, the bathing, and the public groups and I was becoming increasingly fatigued.

Once RJ was asleep at night, we would spend the evening in the bedroom away from the cameras. RJ rarely woke during the night, but we didn't want to complicate this by watching TV in the living area while he slept. Once Jason was asleep I regularly cried myself to sleep. I wanted to scream and live any life but this. It wasn't what I imagined or wanted. My school life had felt like torture, but I'd pray to back to school and be a child again whose only worry was verbal abuse from kids who did it just because they were bored. I wanted a do-over.

After five weeks of being at Cheshire House, we were asked to attend a meeting where staff expressed concern over a few things, like Jason not giving RJ his medication correctly. RJ had been on medication since birth for a thyroid issue, but we had never given him his mediation before, and it was something we'd only learnt when at the foster carer's home. Although this it was something we were both getting used to, other than that they thought Jason was doing well. However, I was charged with not doing enough, letting Jason do too much and not taking charge. I remember thinking to myself 'if only they knew why'. I begged them to give me a little more time, I asked them to tell me straight away if I was doing something wrong because I didn't always see it and if I'm not told then I can't change it because I won't know. I told them I was just struggling being somewhere that wasn't my own house. I came away petrified beyond belief that if I didn't try harder, Jason would get custody of RJ. I had to try and find the energy to drag myself out of the dark well I felt like I was constantly trying but failing to climb out of. RJ needed me to be better.

Over the next few weeks, I tried hard to be more present. I wrote whiteboard tables for meals and drinks and we put up Post-it notes in different places to help me remember things because one of the side effects of my exhaustion was forgetfulness. Putting things in place to improve this was helpful for me and a way to try and focus my attention and create more mindfulness. I tried to speak up more without stepping on Jason' toes. He was so used to being in charge and looking after me because it gave him the position of controller, leader, and power that he seemed to crave. He enjoyed looking good and I was so cautious not to take that from him.

Then out of the blue, the worst happened and as we were lying in bed Jason did what he so often did; only much like the first time I was awake, and he knew it. That night, Jason raped me again in a space where there were audio devices that could hear us, and with our son asleep in the next room. There was no hand over the mouth this time, he knew he wouldn't need it and that I wouldn't make a noise if I could be heard. He knew I was too scared now, my white flag flying high for him signalling my surrender. The whole time he forced himself on me, I lay on my side with his arm over the top of me, pinning me in place. I was staring at the intercom by the door on the bedroom wall. The voice in my head told me that, any moment, I could scream or cry for help and it would be all over. And then I thought of our son in the next room. I thought of how, if I screamed, it would scare him. How, if I indicated in any way as to what Jason was doing to me, it would end with police and reports and judgement. I imagined that they would think that I was a 'Bad Mum' for letting it happen with RJ in the next room, for even coming to Cheshire House, staying with, and marrying someone who would do this. For wanting to bring a baby home to this.

Somewhere along the way I told myself that if we did get RJ home, Jason would stop doing this to me. It was as if I thought he was broken and the only way to fix him would be to bring our son home with us. That night I had the stark realisation of just how wrong I had been. I knew after he was brazened enough to rape me where he could potentially get caught and could have gotten into a lot of trouble, and with RJ in the next room, he was never going to stop. As I often did when he did these things to me, that night I stayed up the whole night thinking over the mess that was my life. I couldn't understand why he would take such a risk this time, maybe he wanted to show me just how much control he had over me, that he knew I wouldn't shout for help, even when I could have. Maybe he just enjoyed the added danger of the possibility of getting caught? The situation mirrored the first time he did this to me and made me realise he had known what he was doing all along. I knew I wasn't ready to leave Jason; I still didn't have the inner strength. I had no choice but to go home with him when our time at Cheshire House came to an end, but I could make sure that RJ didn't have to come home with him. In possibly my first act of genuine love for RJ, I was ready to let him go for his own safety.

The next day it was like I was no longer able to hide that my heart just wasn't in this. I began outwardly showing signs of struggling to cope and being depressed. The staff understood that I could physically do what was needed but could see that I lacked the energy and motivation. It was like I'd just turned off. I was in standby mode. I still worked; I just wasn't switched on right now.

Within a week we had another meeting, and we were told that the assessment had failed, and we were being sent home. Though I appeared upset, the sense of relief in that moment was immense. Still, while it was hard to know that I had failed another son, this time I knew it was for the best. Social Services confirmed they would be asking the Court to release RJ for adoption. Jason was distraught, but he knew there was little we could do now because Cheshire House was our last shot. Jason came away still very reluctant to admit that anything went wrong, and despite both of us knowing we had each made mistakes, Jason couldn't own up to his. I think Jason understood that while I didn't make any mistakes per se, I was wracked with grief and unable to be the mum that RJ needed. Jason believed this was the reason for our failure, which allowed him to redirect any of his own blame onto Social Services. A misdirection for which I was most thankful.

We returned home after only eight weeks of the 12-week assessment completed and continued our weekly contact with RJ, but this began to reduce slowly. Even though the Court released RJ for adoption, Social Services still asked me to visit the same psychologist again. This would be a bonus for them, a way to evidence that my home situation had not improved enough for me to have custody of RJ. This was the route they were taking as to why they were requesting RJ be adopted. My solicitor said I didn't have to have the psychological assessment, but I wanted to see her again because, after Cheshire House, I was having some thoughts that I wanted her professional opinion on.

So, we arranged for her to come to our house around September time and she spoke with both me and Jason together. She asked us how we felt the assessment went and Jason flat out denied any responsibility for any failings on his part. He wasn't the main culprit of the failure, I knew that, but he did do things wrong while we were there, enough so that Social Services weren't considering him for sole custody of RJ, and he wasn't willing or able to see those faults in himself. He lacked the ability to accurately self-reflect, and the psychologist picked up on this, something we later read in her report.

Once she had spoken with us both, I asked if I could talk to her alone; purposefully asking in front of her so that Jason couldn't say no without it looking odd. When he left the room, and I heard his footsteps in the room above, I started to talk to her about the realisations I had with RJ around not bonding with him. I explained to her that I'd recognised now that there was so much that I should never have done, such as trusting someone I had just met with my child. Without saying it outright, I said that there were reasons why the assessment at Cheshire House didn't work out, I understood that it was because I simply didn't try hard enough. I wasn't always present in my mind to give RJ my full self and that there were reasons that could explain this but her knowing them wouldn't change the outcome. However, I wanted her to know that I was aware that these reasons would need addressing when I was ready to do so. I'm sure it all sounded quite vague, but I wanted her opinion on my lack of bond with RJ and she confirmed my thoughts and validated my feelings and explained that it was likely to be expected given everything that had happened.

Upon reading the report several weeks after seeing her, it reflected that I was starting to make some positive changes in my life and my mental health but that I had a long way to go, and it would take years of therapy to overcome my issues. She also noted that she could see a difference in the dynamics of mine and Jason' relationship.

She said in her first report with CJ's proceedings that Jason, after briefly speaking to her over the phone, indicated that I gave the orders in the relationship and it was very much me who led the way and he followed. However, in her second report she admitted that she had this wrong and saw a different side to things now. It was interesting that she picked up on this after I knew in my heart that I needed to leave Jason. I believe I told her this at the time but asked her to leave that out of the report, knowing he would read it.

Jason continued to rape me regularly now that we were home. I never willingly slept with him again. I was still unsure if he knew I was aware of him doing it. I felt like this was all I was worth now. I was hardly ever alone and when I was, I was too scared to reach out to anyone. I didn't even know I was scared anymore because my feelings had shut off and I was just numb. I also hadn't felt pleasure doing anything for a long time.

I had a girl's night out for my best friend's hen party, one of the rare times I was out without Jason, and I spoke to her about wanting to leave Jason. I didn't tell her that he had been raping me, but I told her about me having doubts about him, even before the wedding and that led to me revealing he'd hit me, and I was terrified of trying to leave again. After her wedding, my friend and her husband wanted to help me get out of my home, and my marriage. We came up with a plan for another all-girls night as these tended to be the ones where Jason wouldn't insist on tagging along. This would be a girl's weekend, so I had an excuse to pack a small bag. He seemed a bit taken aback and tried to convince me not to go. I hadn't spent a night away from him since I was in the hospital during our pregnancy with RJ. I was petrified in that moment when I saw his shocked, possibly angry face, that he would stop me from going or say he was coming whether I liked it or not. I played it as cool as I could, promising to message and call him loads, and maybe even sneak out early and come home. This seemed to be enough for him to give his blessing for me to go.

When I got to my friend's house I remember sinking into her sofa, sitting next to her and her husband kneeling in front of me and opening up to them, yet still leaving out the rapes because I didn't want them to say that I was at fault for staying with him and that I never told him to stop. I did tell them about the mental abuse, the control, and the fear I was living in since the pregnancy. I burst into tears, but I was scared to message Jason. I knew I needed to, but I was so worried about what he would do. My friend and her husband were unbelievably kind and gave me the strength and courage I needed to message him. I typed out the words, telling Jason that there was no girls weekend and it had been a way for me to safely get out of the house and that I wouldn't be coming back. For some reason, I apologised for doing it, especially over text. I told him I wanted to break up. It felt like the weight of the entire world had lifted from my shoulders.

It was finally over.

Chapter Sixteen
Independent

Lena and her husband were kind enough to let me stay with them for a few weeks until I went to stay with Mum over Christmas to be closer to family and allow Lena and her husband to have their own space back. I was so happy for the company at a time when I'd lost my way in the world. Leaving Jason, even though I was living life in fear, was still so hard. There was a time when I had relied on him heavily for support. For several years when I wasn't seeing my friends as much, he was the only person in my life who I could talk to. Though he was abusive, and he hurt me more than anyone ever had, he was a constant. I was so used to him arranging our lives, what we would do each day, and his constant presence, that finding my feet alone was much harder than I had anticipated. In trying to build some bridges before ending the relationship, I had joined a local amateur dramatic pantomime. I carried this on once we split as I had a responsibility to continue as I was the leading lady. I hadn't participated in singing or acting since school, and I hadn't been the leading lady since I was Cinderella in our college panto, just before I dropped out when I was in the throes of puppy love with Matthew. I felt alive to be doing something I loved again, even if I was a bag of nerves.

Almost a month after abruptly leaving Jason, I returned to my old home with Mum to collect my things. I'd asked Jason to gather them ahead of me picking them up and he graciously agreed. We'd been in very little contact since I left, because when we did talk, he always wanted it to be about getting back together and trying again. I wasn't interested. He was stand-offish and short-tempered when I saw him, probably because I wasn't alone so he couldn't say or do anything. The living room was a mess and he had someone staying with him now. He was never one for being alone, so it didn't surprise me. Oddly, despite still fearing him, I also cared for him and was glad he wasn't alone. I'm not sure why I felt that way after everything he did. I found it difficult to not have empathy for him. Perhaps it sprung from making excuses for him for so long, that he would just always have this hold on me. After leaving him, even I was thankful for company, as it had been easier than I imagined for him to get back into my head simply by standing there in front of me. I was glad that he wasn't aware of how much power my subconscious had given him. The only time I saw Jason after that was at any court dates that we still needed to attend in relation to RJ's adoption. There were still a few before his adoption order would be made final.

Continuing my surge towards independence, I applied for a job as the head waitress at a small café in Skipton. The building used to house the café where I worked with Lena when we'd just left school in 2004-2005. We used to have such a good time there. I think the fact that I had worked in the tearoom that was there before it, is the reason I got the job. It was only a small space, a very narrow building that you wouldn't think would be big enough for much. There were only around seven tables, but they would often be full, so it was tough work by myself. The café was split into sections over the three floors. On the ground floor was where my boss worked, he did the beverages for take away customers and for the customers who ate in, so I'd have to go down and bring them back up to serve. My boss' wife was the chef and she was on the top floor, up a further two flights of stairs, and I'd have to go up and down those for the food. I worked nine-hour days and most of that would be spent going up and down across all three floors, carrying drinks and heavy plates of food, and clearing tables afterwards. I lost a lot of weight doing this job, and it was certainly the fittest I'd ever felt. I worked there five or six days a week and it felt good to be out of the house each day and doing something for myself in a productive way. However, being the only waitress and working full time soon burnt me out and I was unable to keep up the pace, and I stayed until after Christmas, giving them time to find my replacement.

A couple of weeks later, and with a little financial help from Mum, I moved into my very first house alone. It was in the same village that I did the panto in, so I knew the area and although I didn't know anyone who lived there, it didn't feel a million miles from Skipton; just a bus ride away. I couldn't afford anything by myself in Skipton, but I was eager to get out from under Mum's roof. It was hard to go back home after living away for so long. I yearned for somewhere to call my own again. It was an end terrace, one bedroomed house and parts of it were snug, but it was just right for me and I could make it my own. I was happy here, having my own little place to call home was something I thought I wouldn't like, but I enjoyed having my own space and not having to answer to anyone much more than I ever thought I would.

I had been speaking to Jason a lot in the last few months and it was looking like we had settled into a friendship. We decided to meet up, and him and Alex came round to help me decorate my bedroom. At the time I was feeling quite lonely, and Jason had said all the right things to make me think he had changed. He was the man I saw when we first met. At the very least, I thought that maybe we could attempt to be friends; given our history and it would be good that we could remain amicable for RJ's sake.

They came around and we all spent the day working hard and painting and we didn't finish until late so they both stayed over. We ordered out and chatted about old times. Jason' charm was certainly working on me, and I came so very close to giving in and trying again. If Alex hadn't been there, it might have ended differently. Instead, I realised I could never go back to Jason. The next day I told him this, to his disappointment. I'd had too many sleepless nights, too many nightmares, and tried too hard to build myself back up again, for me to turn around and walk backwards now.

I never saw Jason again after that, this closed the chapter on a part of my life that I deeply regretted; that I had learnt so much from yet was still very much hurting from too. Walking away from the possibility of being with Jason again made me realise that I was starting to believe in myself again, a belief that I deserved more than the kind of relationship that centred around his gratification and greed, and his need to control everything. I was ready to be a partner, and not a silent one, an equal one. I knew this was something that Jason couldn't give. This goodbye was one I offered freely, and it felt empowering.

Chapter Seventeen
Goodbye RJ

While I was building up my life of independence and trying to find myself again, contact with RJ had been reduced but ongoing. I was now seeing him around once a month, but this month was to be our last. As he never came home, and despite having a short few months with him where I was with him 24/7, RJ had never bonded to me. It's not surprising given the circumstances. I was also never truly able to find my motherly bond to him either. Though I loved him deeply, I knew the outcome was for the best. We made the most of the times we did see him, and I always visited with Mum and Lisa. After returning from Cheshire House, RJ was placed with a different foster placement and contact was moved closer to where he was staying. As I didn't drive my Mum would always take us in her car, and it was good to not have contacts alone given that I struggled to bond with RJ. It took the pressure off me being the only one in the room.

Now it was time to say goodbye. Another 'see you later' for my family. Another permanent reminder of my failure to be a Mum. This time, however, I had the relief of knowing that RJ was going to be in a safer and much better place. Once the placement had finished at Cheshire House and Social Services discussed the next steps with me, one of the first things I had asked was whether Peggy and Chris wanted to adopt RJ too. I was overjoyed when word came back a couple of weeks later to say that they did. My boys would grow up together, the way they always would have, just without me there. At least they would have each other. This solidified the feeling that this was how things were meant to turn out. It made saying goodbye a little easier, knowing he was going to lovely parents.

During the process of the adoption, we worked on RJ's life story book. As before, I gathered the few things I did have, which were mostly from his days in the NICU, along with anything we had bought him thinking he'd be coming home. We sent him with two very large teddies. One from Jason' mum and the other from my Grandad. CJ also had one from my Grandad, so it was a tradition. Most of the things I had, I kept in the memory box along with CJ's things. All small, insignificant items to most people but ones that meant a lot to me. We had little toys that were his favourites, once upon a time, and little craft projects that we all did at Cheshire House when we knew the assessment had failed. I had hospital bands, photos and even his empty medicine bottle. From what I kept it was obvious that there was always some connection deep down that I hadn't allowed myself to feel, but it felt like there was little point in trying to find it now, on our last day.

On the day, we decided it was best to only have myself, Mum, and Lisa at the goodbye this time given that RJ never got to know anyone else. We sat and played with him for a few hours. I think we played with almost every toy there. This time didn't feel the same though. We'd done this before; we knew he wasn't bonded to us and, with RJ never having spent time at home, and this being a possibility from the start, I think everyone had prepared for this eventuality and so it wasn't quite as emotional. Still, the hours passed and for a while we forgot and just enjoyed his company. His cheeky little grin, his happy eyes and adventurous personality. We took our final photos, and then came the tears when we wound down to leave, when we knew our time was up. I had my final hug, but I had no words for him, other than to tell him I loved him and that I was sorry.

Chapter Eighteen
Trauma

On Valentine's Day 2009, I went on a date with someone I'd met through doing the pantomime. It went well, and he dropped me off afterwards. As I walked up my path and unlocked my door someone jumped over my garden wall, ran toward me, and tried to get into my house. Reacting quickly, I had managed to get inside but upon closing my door I had trapped the man's leg in the door so it wouldn't close. He threatened me with a knife to let him in, but when I wouldn't take my weight off the door he managed to pull it out and ran away. I called the police after the shock had worn off but when they came around they refused to believe what had happened. I was dumbfounded by the fact that these police officers came into my house and refused to believe that someone had attempted to break in. When they wouldn't leave until I told them 'the truth' I ended up making up a lie about owing someone money, which they accepted as truth immediately, and they left with no further action taken.

Later that night I messaged my date to tell him what had happened and the next day he messaged me to say he no longer wanted to go out with me as there was too much drama in my life. Not for the first time, I felt let down by someone who should have been there for me, and I felt very alone in the world again.

Almost a year to the day since the attempted break in I came home after going shopping. As I went to unlock my door, I noticed it was already unlocked and I was angry at myself, assuming I had left it open all day. I closed and locked the door behind me and walked into the living room and over to the corner, where I placed my shopping bags on the floor and began taking off my coat. Suddenly my breath caught, and I froze as I heard footsteps in the room behind me. I swung around but as I did someone grabbed me around my waist. A scuffle ensued and he overpowered me; pulling my top and bra off over my head and throwing me to the floor, he then removed my trousers and underwear, leaving me completely naked. He flipped me onto my stomach and with his knee on my back he gagged me with a piece of duct tape. I screamed but it was impossible to generate any great volume. He tied my hands behind me with a cable tie, so I couldn't move to fight him off. I couldn't see his face, nor did I want to. I listened as he stood up and switched the main lights on in the room. I instantly shut my eyes. The fear of seeing him gripped me. I'd seen so many shows and films that gave the impression that if you see an attacker and you can identify them, then they will need to kill you. I heard him slowly taking off his clothes, he turned me onto my back then climbed on top of me and raped me. It seemed to last forever. As it was going on, I remember briefly opening my eyes and looking at a photo of CJ and RJ hanging on my wall. I wondered at what point did my life turn in to this constant hell.

The carpet began burning the skin on my arms and I focused on that instead of the sensation of him moving in and out of me. The pain of his roughness searing through my body, pinned down by his weight, the mental pain so much worse than the carpet burns. Tears were trickling down my face, and I struggled to breathe through them. Still careful not to look at who ever this man was, I turned to see his shoes on the floor. Olive green canvas shoes with white laces and brown soles. I stared at them until he was done, all the while crying and begging for him to stop. When he was done, I closed my eyes and wished for the world to end.

When it was over, he laughed, got up and put his clothes back on then he knelt and pushed me onto my stomach. He untied me and took off my gag. After trying so hard, not to look at him, through teary blurred vision that slowly cleared, I accidentally caught sight of him, only to realise that it was the man who had tried to break in last year. He ordered me to stay laying down until he had gone and reminded me that if I ever told anyone what happened, he knew where to find me. Curling into a ball I laid there naked for a long while, too scared to move. Then I realised my front door was unlocked and I grabbed the throw from the sofa and wrapped it around myself so I could go into the porch and lock the door. I walked upstairs and crawled into my bed where I stayed awake all night, too petrified to close my eyes.

The next day, I was too scared to go to the police, but I knew there were places I could call and ended up going to a trauma centre a few hours away from where I lived. I travelled by myself on a train, on auto pilot, just doing what I thought needed to be done. I told them what had happened, and they took photos of the marks and swabs for DNA. While I was giving them my statement, my Mum called. She had texted earlier in the day and I had ignored it, which wasn't like me. She could tell something was wrong, despite my efforts to convince her otherwise over the phone. I couldn't lie to her, so I told her what had happened and where I was, and I think I heard her heart break through the phone.

Mum and Lisa met me at the station on my return and I threw myself into their arms while we all cried together on the station platform for several minutes. I didn't want to talk to them about it and shared only the basics of what had happened. They drove me back to my home and stayed for a while. Mum wanted to stop with me that night, but I put my foot down and told her no. If I needed her that night, what would I do the next? I was alone the night it happened, and I somehow got through it, so I knew I could do it. I needed space and time right now. I told her I was fine, and she was only a phone call away if I needed her. She begged me to go to the police but given that I harboured a deep hatred for them, blaming my rape on their lack of belief the year before, I didn't have much hope that it would do any good, so I didn't report it.

Over the next few days, I had nightmares, I was terrified of walking around my own house, and I needed to leave the lights on because I was now afraid of the dark. I became obsessed with checking my doors were locked, and for a while I even put things in front of them until I realised if I could lift whatever it was in front of my door, then someone could still get through the door.

The trauma centre I went to offered me eight weeks of one-to-one counselling that they come to your house to carry out, which I accepted and, although it didn't scratch the surface, it allowed me to get through things much better just knowing I could talk about it with someone. I was also given the opportunity to have someone from the police come to speak to me, off the record, about what happened, and they talked me through what the process would be if I decided to report it. After learning what had happened, they said that their experience told them the man had probably been watching me for some time, which meant he was likely to be a local. They said it was likely that this person knew me from somewhere, and even if I didn't know them, I'd probably have seen them at some point or passed them by.

Mum repeatedly asked me to move, but I was so stubborn about it. I had lost so much already, had so much taken from me against my wishes, CJ and RJ, Jason raping me and taking my freedom, and now this. I didn't want this man to take my home from me. It was the first place I'd ever been independent, and I was reluctant to give it up. At this point, my home felt like all I had left. If I ever moved, I wanted it to be on my terms, and not because I was running away.

This event, understandably, severely affected Mum and she was beside herself with worry about it for a long time after the attack. I began pushing the mental torment I was experiencing into the box in my mind and feigning a version of normality for Mum. Seeing me feeling better and smiling more gave her a reason to move on from it, not truly knowing how much this had broken me. After a while of pretending to be okay for Mum, I started to believe it myself and a strong denial of the trauma I had suffered overrode my life.

Chapter Nineteen
We Meet Again

A few months after saying our goodbyes to RJ, I was sent a letter to say that Peggy and Chris wanted to see me again. They also asked if Mum and Lisa would like to meet them too. I was so happy to hear from them, happier still to hear that they would like to meet up again, so I could get an update about the boys. I was so unbelievably grateful that they would want to meet two of the most important people in my life as well. I'd spent so long telling Mum and Lisa how lovely they were, and now they would find out for themselves. I knew this wasn't likely the norm for a closed adoption and this made it even more special. Telling them both that they would get to meet Peggy and Chris was great and they were excited for the opportunity.

We arranged through Social Services to have the meeting at an office building not too far from where we lived. Two social workers came but they gave us space to get to know one another and pretty much stayed out of the way, but within ear shot should they need to step in. We had our introductions and Peggy and Chris started telling us how RJ was settling in. It was lovely to hear that he was happy and doing well with them, more so that he and CJ were getting along, although I'm sure it was an adjustment. We all had a drink, and I allowed Mum and Lisa to get to know them since I'd already met them. I took a bit of a back seat to allow them all to ask questions and build rapport. About an hour into the meeting, they explained they had brought a short home movie of the boys for us to watch. I wasn't aware of this ahead of time and suddenly my heart started racing. I would get to see the boys moving and interacting. I'd never seen them in the same room together.

As we watched the videos I felt a lump in my throat upon hearing the boys speak. CJ more than RJ, but even RJ was babbling a lot more than he had. Hearing what CJ sounded like was a painful elation for me. I was incredibly pleased to have finally heard what he sounded like, but it was with an aching heart that I knew this was all I could get. I was beyond grateful, I never imagined I would even have a video, and the fact that I was watching him on screen was overwhelming. Something that so many wouldn't think that you would miss after forced adoption is hearing your child's voice. Maybe their smile, hugging them, or generally just being with them. But I had never heard CJ speak and it was something I'd always wondered how he would sound. I dreamt about him often, but they were silent dreams because my mind couldn't fill in the missing sound. Now I had it, they were giving me a gift without even knowing how much it meant to me. I started to cry, instantly apologising, and feeling embarrassed in case I made them feel bad for bringing the video. That wasn't my intention at all. I explained and they understood. Peggy was so caring and supportive of how I felt. I spent a lot of time always doing my best to consider Peggy and Chris' feelings and ensuring I never said anything to hurt them in anyway or devalue their importance in all of this. It felt very much like Peggy was doing the same in that moment. It served to bolster the already enormous amount of respect I had for them both.

A little before the end of the meeting, Peggy and Chris handed us some items from the boys such as photos, writing, and craft projects. In with mine was a little piece of paper with a handwritten email address. As they passed this to me they said they wanted us to start emailing each other, if this was something that I would feel comfortable with and was open to trying out. Though we had all been taking part in letterbox contact, which was one letter and a photo of each of the boys per year (although we hadn't gotten one with RJ yet), they said it would be easier get to know one another without having to go through an intermediary service. They felt comfortable enough with me to create a separate email account, specifically for us to be able to communicate back and forth, in the hope of building our relationship.

If you could have seen the look on the social workers' faces; it was one of the funniest things ever. Wide eyed and flapping around like penguins, panicking because even though they heard what we were saying, they had no power to stop it from happening. I was hesitant at first, waiting for one of them to jump in and say I wasn't allowed to do it, but they never did and so I accepted it. I was in such shock that they felt open to this and honoured they cared enough, though it did cross my mind a few times that maybe they were simply being polite and didn't actually want me to email them. That self-doubt always creeping back in.

Before we left we took a photo of all of us together so Peggy and Chris could show the boys and we could have a copy too. On the drive home Mum and Lisa repeatedly stated how nice they both were and that they came away feeling how I'd felt the first time I met them, with a sense of closure that made them feel more at ease knowing the boys were safe, happy, and loved with a lovely family. The meeting couldn't have gone any better. This meeting had been such a productive and overwhelming few hours, but one that would set the course for my future and I had no idea at the time.

I didn't rush home to send my first email. In fact, I over thought the situation entirely and became too scared to email at all. I didn't want to get my hopes up in case it was somehow taken away by Social Services. I wasn't sure if they could do that, was it worth the risk of starting something only to have it taken away and feel another sense of loss all over again?

I'd already almost lost contact altogether after I posted photos on my social media that Peggy and Chris had given me at our first meeting. When Social Services found out about this, and I'm not sure how they did, I was sent a strongly worded letter ordering me to take them down or I would never get another photo. I hadn't realised I wasn't allowed to post photos of the boys, even from the times I saw them before they were adopted. I questioned whether I wanted to step into a situation where I could risk the wrath of Social Services again? Besides, I was also clueless about how to start the email. I didn't want to be too informal, but I didn't want to come across like I was writing to them without emotion. I didn't want to overstep any boundaries and I wondered if emailing at all was overstepping. What if they gave it to me, but didn't genuinely want me to take them up on their offer?

In August, we received our letters from the Letterbox and this year at the end of mine there was a postscript that invited me to use the email should I wish to. It was the gentle nudge I needed to send my first email to Peggy and Chris. In it, I simply thanked them for their letter and the photos of the boys, adding that I hoped they were all well. I signed off with my name, two kisses and a smiley face. As soon as I sent it, I worried that the sign off was too much. Were kisses appropriate? I expected either no reply, or one that asked me not to do that again. I assumed I had blown my first ever attempt to email them and open conversation.

A week passed and I didn't hear back. Negative thoughts rushed through my brain; I must have definitely said something wrong, or I was right in thinking that they didn't actually want to have email contact with me. I felt silly for having gotten my hopes up. However, a fortnight after sending my email, a reply came in from Peggy apologising for the late reply and explaining they'd not had internet access for the last few weeks. (This was back in the day before people had regular email access through their phones.) She then gave a little snippet of information about the boys and said they were looking forward to receiving my letter. She signed off 'Best wishes, Peggy x'. I won't lie, seeing a kiss at the end of the message brought such relief to me. Now I knew we were on the same page I felt much more comfortable responding.

At first our communications tended to be short little messages, partly because we were getting to know one another. We told each other about our days, and I'd maybe hear a little about the boys. On the odd occasion the boys would ask to send a little message to me. It was lovely to hear that Peggy and Chris had chosen to be fully open with CJ and RJ about being adopted and they referred to me as 'Mummy Laura'. As we continued to email, we started exchanging birthday greetings and holiday messages. I was careful at first, to keep it simple and I let them lead, and it worked for us. The ice was well and truly broken, and we were doing contact our way.

Chapter Twenty

Stewart

Despite everything I had been through, I still wanted to find my Mr Right. Life was so far from the teen movies I used to look to for love advice, it was never close to the fairy tale I had hoped it would be, but I still had dreams of finding 'the one'. Somehow, I still believed in love, I just wasn't in a rush to find it. I'd done so much at such a young age, and I wanted to enjoy my life and just go where the wind was taking me. I had tried dating here and there with someone I'd met while out with friends as well as another guy I'd met online but distance got in the way. I wasn't looking for anything serious but if something had come along then I'd have been more than happy. I edited my online dating profile after distance became an issue and I changed it to read 'If you don't live close to me then please don't message me'. I forgot about the site for a month and when I came back to it in April the first message I read was from a guy called Stewart. It started with 'I live exactly 5.7 miles from you, is that close enough?'. It made me chuckle for the first time in a long time, so I messaged him back.

Stewart and I seemed to get along and so we swapped numbers after a few back-and-forth messages online. We started to message each other every day and we added each other on Facebook, mostly to prove we were real people. He'd been a regular poster for a few years, had not too many but not too few friends to seem suspicious, and his photos appeared to match how he described himself. No alarm bells were ringing, thankfully. He lived in Silsden, where I used to live with Jason when I was pregnant with RJ, so it was good to know he was a local guy and within a reasonable travelling distance. I didn't want to rush things, but I knew it would be better to meet up and carry things on in person, rather than dragging things out online. A couple of days after my 22nd birthday, we arranged to meet in Skipton. We didn't have a lot in common, but his personality drew me in, and from the photos I'd seen, he was good looking. I was excited, but nervous.

The day of our meeting was a beautiful day, quite warm for the time of year. I tried on several different outfits, in fact, practically most of my wardrobe. I landed on a beautiful deep blue silk dress with an intricate gold pattern all over it. The dress had straps and although it was quite busty, because of the design it didn't look cheap or tacky in anyway. It flowed out from under the bust and was short around the mid-thigh area. It had a blue sequin band under the bust. I wore a blue cardigan, which I kept unfastened. I had never liked my arms so I generally kept them covered up and I knew it would get cooler as the night went on. I styled my hair half up and half down, my current favourite style after I had recently cut my hair for a nice change. It was the shortest it had been since I was in school, just about shoulder length.

Mum and Lisa came to see me before the date and drove me back to Skipton because public transport wasn't regular in my little village. Mum repeatedly asked if I wanted her to come with me to meet Stewart, to which I of course said no. She offered to simply walk behind me instead, and I again politely declined. I knew she meant well, and it made me laugh and relax a little, but I wanted to do this myself.

I walked into Wetherspoons and noticed Stewart standing up in the far corner of the room and waving me over. He was very handsome and had a big, bright smile, which was the first thing I noticed. Stewart's hair was very dark brown that was almost black, and it was short but styled into spikes. His eyes had a ring of light brown around the pupil surrounded by a pool of greyish blue. He was clean shaven and had freckles on his cheeks. Looking smart dressed in black leather style shoes, dark blue jeans that looked new, and a white t-shirt under a thick charcoal cardigan. He had good taste and I was immediately impressed.

We sat down and I could tell he seemed nervous too, which made me feel slightly better because I knew it meant he cared enough about us meeting to be nervous. We'd spoken a lot online, so we skipped the awkward chit chat at the start, where neither of you knows what to say, and our conversation flowed easily. We talked about hobbies and what he did for work. I spoke about the pantomimes I'd been in and shared that I'd recently taken up running and was entering the Great North Run. I told him about my last job that was very briefly at a phone store over the last summer, this led us on to talking about phones and tech. We stayed in the same bar all night getting to know each other. We laughed and never once ran out of things to say, Stewart was just so easy to speak to. I could imagine us not just as boyfriend and girlfriend, but good friends too. When it was time to leave, he walked me to the local taxi station, and we went home in separate taxis. He messaged me on the way home to say he had a great night and couldn't wait to see me again. I remember smiling the rest of the night.

A week later, we arranged to go bowling together in Leeds. We spoke a little in between via text or Facebook. Competition was always good on a date because it brings out a little bit of natural flirty behaviour in me, the playful side of me that doesn't think about things too much. While we ate, we took the chance to keep chatting and he asked if I had kids. This seemed a bit out of the blue to ask, until I realised we were Facebook friends, so he'd probably seen a post where I'd spoken about the boys, as I sometimes did around their birthdays. I explained in as few words as I could, that I had two boys, but they no longer lived with me and were now adopted. Without going into too much detail, more than aware that I didn't want to scare him off, I told him about Social Services and why the boys weren't returned to my care. I stressed that I did not cause the injury, something I was always worried about telling people. I had never gotten to a point of needing to mention it to anyone I'd dated but Stewart asked, and I didn't want to lie. Surprisingly, when I told him, he wasn't put off in the slightest. He went on to further shock me by saying a member of his family had had a similar experience but was luckily able to get custody back. I think this allowed him to be more open minded about the whole situation, and I was so thankful.

In the following weeks, we went on several more dates and it was going well. I liked him a lot and he just seemed like this genuinely normal, everyday guy who was funny and great company. In May, we enjoyed our first kiss and then we made our relationship 'official', which of course for our generation meant that we each updated our Facebook status to being 'in a relationship'. Stewart had been so kind in taking things at my own pace, never once pushing me past my comfort zone. I had told him about Jason, and the attack, before we met, though I didn't go into the detailed specifics. I had wanted to kiss him many times in the past few weeks, but I didn't want to rush into it, and he was very respectful of this, something that made me think highly of him. After a short while I met his family and his beautiful dog, Havoc, who was his best friend. I started to stay over at his Mum's with him and he stayed at mine every now and then too. I introduced him to my Mum who had been dying to meet him. We took our time and just enjoyed each other's company.

In July, he went away with work over the period of his birthday and when he returned he came to celebrate at my house, and this was the first time we said 'I love you' to one another. It was a big step to say it for me, the last time I had said this to anyone was when I was with Jason. I wanted to make sure that the next time I said it, would be the last person I ever said it to. Not to get too ahead of myself, I already had a feeling that me and Stewart were in it for the long haul together. I wanted to make sure that the next time I said those words, it was to someone who I felt safe and comfortable with. For the first time in years, I felt that with Stewart.

It was around this time that I knew that I wanted to move out of the house I was in and move somewhere closer to either my family or Stewart. I still didn't have a job so I knew I still wouldn't get somewhere in Skipton, so I chose to look for something in Silsden, close to Stewart. Even though I knew it would be a while yet, the hope was that we would one day move in together and when that time came, I knew this would be in Silsden as he had a solid, long term job in Silsden, and he didn't drive. It wouldn't be fair to expect him to move elsewhere for me, especially if I still wasn't working. Providing I was close to him, that's all I cared about.

In August, I was accepted for a small one bedroom, second floor flat in an old converted Methodist chapel with beautiful views across the countryside. There was a nice living room with an archway to the open kitchen. The bedroom was much smaller than the one at the house, but it was still big enough for the bed and my furniture. The bathroom was off the hallway as you walked into the flat. It was small but perfect and the view made it worth it. Decorated completely in magnolia, with an older style kitchen, it felt cosy and was perfect for Stewart to come around whenever he wanted. He'd typically spend a few evenings and all weekend with me, and Havoc would come stay over the weekend too which I loved. We would go for walks, go bowling or to play pool, or sometimes we'd just stay in and watch a film together.

Our first Christmas together, on Christmas Eve we sat down together and watched Home Alone and agreed to make it a tradition, and he stayed the night. My family all had flu that year, so I spent Christmas Day with Stewart and his family. We all had a lovely day, though it was the first Christmas I had ever spent away from my own family, being with Stewart made up for that. His family had always been so nice and welcoming, and it was lovely to spend it watching his niece's and nephew open their gifts. I was thankful to be asked to spend the day with them.

Spending any day around children was always hard but thankfully very rare for me, spending Christmas with Stewart's family I couldn't help but think what it would have been like to have a child with me at Christmas. The children were quick to warm up to me and spent the day coming to talk to me and hug me and aside from my own nephew, it was the first time I'd been so close to children since having the boys and it was a little overwhelming. In my mind, as I hugged them and as they sat on my knee and watched Fireman Sam for the umpteenth time that day, it was hard not to picture them as CJ or RJ, to think what it would have been like to have them on my knee on Christmas morning opening presents, excited about which one to open first and jumping up and down when they opened that one gift they wanted above all others.

Luckily, with three kids in the house that day it was easy to get distracted and so I didn't dwell on my thoughts for long. Stewart and I had our first New Year's at a local bar together and I felt positive about the year ahead. Now I had Stewart, I wanted to move forward with a new hope that better things were to come.

Chapter Twenty-One
Growth

To continue forwards with my life, the first thing on my agenda was to book an appointment with the solicitor and start divorce proceedings. I was starting to feel more like myself, now I wanted my name back.

Stewart and I had many plans for 2011, then the world decided to throw us a curve ball. Unexpectedly, we found out a few days into the New Year that we were pregnant. I was scared because of my history with Social Services that, yet again, not enough time had passed for the outcome to be different. I was also unsure if this was something we were ready for. We'd been together less than a year and this was certainly not in our plan. I was nervous to tell Stewart, wondering how he might react. It wasn't that I expected him to be angry, but I also didn't know him well enough to say whether he would run for the hills or not. To my relief he was very supportive about it and he said he'd stand by me all the way. I knew then that I had truly found a good man. Once the shock had passed we told our families and while they were happy, they were clearly a little stunned at the news. We understood, given the circumstances.

The prospect of being a mum again filled me with dread for many reasons, but I hoped this time would be different, and I felt ready to face the challenge head on. I had always wanted to be a mum though, so ultimately I was overjoyed. No sooner had we all let the notion of a new baby sink in than, during the fifth week of the pregnancy, I miscarried. I was broken hearted. Miscarriage is something that everyone is aware of, but for some reason you never believe it will happen to you. The loss brought me and Stewart closer and he was such a comfort in the days after finding out. A few days later he came to see me after work and brought me some daffodils, my favourite flower, and an American dollar bill.

One of my biggest dreams, other than being a mum, was wanting to visit New York. It wasn't just a dream, but something I'd always felt destined to do. Though I'd never been, whenever I would see New York on the TV or see an image of it, it felt familiar to me somehow. I felt like I belonged there. I'd been this way for as long as I could remember. I know that it most likely came from the fact that a lot of the teen movies I watched in my childhood tended to be set there and it was always portrayed as this amazing place where people's dreams come true. I wanted to believe it was something else drawing me there though. Fate, maybe. Stewart gave me the dollar bill because we often discussed going to New York one day, and he wanted to remind me that I still had other dreams that we could reach for. We had all the time in the world to start a family.

In February, after being in my little flat for six months, I moved into another flat in the same building, quite possibly the shortest move ever. My previous flat had severe damp and mould issues, so I needed to vacate it while it was fixed, and I chose not to return. The new flat was far more modern having been recently renovated and was about the same size although with a slightly different layout, and it was on the ground floor, so I lost the beautiful views of the sprawling countryside. However, to make up for that, I did get the only flat in the building with outdoor space. The kitchen had a door that opened onto a little patio which was a little bonus feature.

Later that year, having gained more confidence and feeling ready to put myself out there, I started my first proper full-time job, and I was thrilled to be doing something productive with my time again, not to mention earning money again. I worked for a claim's management company doing data entry. It was simple to pick up and made the day pass by in a flash. Another benefit was that I had the opportunity to meet new people and make some friends, something I felt was lacking after losing touch with my friends in Skipton. I still saw them when me and Stewart first met but the more time I spent with him I just seemed to drift apart from them. Not in a negative way, my friends were now all meeting people and settling down just as I was, so it was more of a natural parting of ways when life sometimes gets in the way.

It was around this time that I heard from Peggy, CJ and RJ's adoptive mum. Email contact had been going steadily with us even though at first I had felt a little reluctant to use it, and despite being hugely grateful to be given this method of contact. I had to wrestle a lot with my inner monologue to feel worthy of having the opportunity, when so many other birth families don't get anything. While life had gotten busy on me, the boys were never far from my mind. I'd email on birthdays and at Christmas. Peggy and I had found our flow in messaging each other, it suited us well and we'd connected as friends too, often sending messages just to have a natter to one another. This email was about the boys though, an email I had never anticipated would come, at least not so soon.

Our communications outside of letterbox contact enabled me to get to know Peggy, Chris, and the boys as the family they were, and allowed the boys to be inquisitive, particularly CJ as he was a little older. Peggy explained in her email that CJ had recently been expressing a want to see me, and not just as a passing thought. They ran this past their social worker and enquired about how best to handle this and the advice given was, in short, that it was up to them. However, they were advised to wait a year and see if the thoughts were fleeting. Nobody wanted to rush into this, if this were to happen then it would only go ahead if all of us were ready and willing, and they were sure it was right for the boys. I didn't let myself get too excited, or too nervous, fully understanding that with CJ being five years old at the time, he might change his mind, and that was okay, that's a kid's prerogative. So, I waited. Tentatively.

I couldn't help but imagine what it would be like to see the boys again. I dreamed about it often enough, even before now. I would always picture that movie moment where someone is reunited, and it happens in slow motion. Seeing each other across a field, or from a distance, they leap into your arms and you embrace. I never allowed myself to believe it would happen, not until they were adults at the very least, but I couldn't stop my dreams from showing me what my true hopes were. My dreams never lied, never stopped wanting that reunion sooner rather than later.

When CJ and RJ were taken from me, I could have spent my whole life pining for them. I could have hit the pause button and never done anything with my life until they were a part of it again. But what would they have thought when they came to find me, only to see someone who was too broken by her loss that she never got to live? I wanted to have stories to tell them, tales of the adventures I'd had while I knew they were off having their own with their incredible family. I wanted to be able to tell them that I made the best of my life, but always kept them close to my heart. It's a very individual choice how someone chooses to handle their grief, and I dealt with mine by choosing to live. This isn't to say that I wasn't far more emotionally scarred by losing the boys than I'd admitted to even myself, but I'd locked away the pain in the box in my mind a long time ago. I focused on the positives, I put in the effort to stay in contact in every way possible and now I could potentially be getting the reward.

At the back end of the year, I received a final letter from my solicitor with my decree absolute. I was officially divorced, and I could finally put an end to one of the worst chapters of my life. 2011 may have started with the agonising pain of Stewart and I losing our first baby together, but there had certainly been many things since to make up for it and allow me to feel positive about my future.

Chapter Twenty-Two
Reunion

New Year 2012 came and went and in a wicked repeat of the previous year, with Stewart and I suffering another loss. Sadly, once you've had one miscarriage you fear another and so it wasn't altogether unexpected. Even though I knew they shouldn't be happening, being the pessimist I am, I had been telling myself since the day I saw those two lines on the test, that I would have another loss. The very fact that I did only served to further confirm my self-deprecating thoughts that I was a bad person and didn't deserve to have another baby because I wasn't a good enough mum to the two boys I already had. This was absolutely what my subconscious told me on an almost daily basis, but too dark of a thought to maintain without reaching breaking point, I locked it away with everything else in the box in my mind that was near capacity.

After going through another loss, and in desperate need of some good news, Stewart and I decided it was time to take the next step in our relationship and move in together. In February, we found a beautiful, three-bedroom house in the town where we were living. There was one bedroom for us, the second for a home office or games room as we both had computers and played games together. The box room, which was still a great size, was a spare room for Stewart's nieces and nephew or other family to stay in. It was a terraced house, and the rooms were large. The windows let in lots of light, very different from where I was living before. We felt excited to be moving in together, Stewart had only ever lived away from home for a very short period, so he was like a giddy kid at Christmas.

We hadn't long since moved into the new house when I received an email from Peggy. She told me that CJ was still asking to meet, and she felt we should probably start to put some plans in place to make it happen. I had to be gentle with my heart and keep it safe, especially where the boys were concerned. The meeting was completely about them, but I couldn't ignore the very significant mental affect it would have on me. We moved forward with the planning, but I always half expected it to be cancelled before it could happen. Peggy suggested that she and I meet beforehand to talk things though and we answer any questions the other had. She felt it was better done in person and would allow us to see each other again before the big day itself. The reunion with the boys was set for July so we could be more hopeful of good weather. So, in early July I met up with Peggy in Skipton. We talked about where the boys were at, and what CJ had been specifically saying when asking to see me. I found out that RJ had some reservations and so I was aware that on the day, if he didn't want to go ahead with meeting me, or he wanted to stop at any time, then his Dad would take him off to spend time with him alone. Both mine and Peggy's priority were the boys and them being comfortable with everything and taking it at their pace. Their needs were front and centre at all times.

I was so thankful to have met with Peggy prior to seeing the boys, to make sure we both knew the ins and outs of what would happen and to ensure we were on the same page. I was still gobsmacked that these two wonderful parents would even want me to be in the boys' lives; I couldn't help but think about how this would be for them and I always made sure to check that they were okay with it. We were friends now and I didn't want to jeopardise that. Peggy and Chris had rented a beautiful house in Hebden Bridge for a week and the plan we agreed was for me to go to house, and if everything went well and the boys responded positively, Mum and Lisa would then join me for a second visit a few days later.

When I told Mum, she would be seeing the boys again, she wept down the phone. Lisa was ecstatic to be seeing them again too. I often forgot too easily, in my little grief bubble, that this affected my family as well. They also lost the boys, and it was unlike anything our family had ever gone through before. The most we ever spoke of the boys was either on their birthdays and at Christmas. Their presence in the family was missed often, but particularly on days that would have been all about them. Losing the boys may possibly have been the most tragic event to happen to my immediate family and if just telling them about it was a happy day, I couldn't wait to see them reunite with each other.

I was so nervous in the lead up to the seeing the boys. It seemed strange that someone would be dreading seeing their own flesh and blood, but I was. I feared them not liking me. I knew they likely had an image built up in their minds of who I was, and I was so scared that I wouldn't even come close to measuring up to their idea of me.

On the morning of the big day, I was barely able to function normally. I cried a lot, and I was, admittedly, a little snappy with Stewart. I remember telling him to ignore everything I said, I was just a little hysterical. I wasn't happy with what I was wearing or how I looked, but there was little I could do about that now. Stewart travelled with me on the train to see me off and meet up with me at the end of the day. Bless him for wandering around some random little town for hours on end just so I didn't have to be alone. We got to the train station and Peggy was waiting to take me to the house they had rented specifically to ensure the space was pleasant and enjoyable, rather than a Social Services office.

The house stood atop a very steep hill overlooking the valley below. As we pulled up, I couldn't decide what would give out first, my knees or my heart. I saw both the boys stood outside to greet us. CJ was jumping up and down, RJ was waiting with his Dad and keeping back, still a little unsure. CJ ran over to the car and stood there as I opened the door. We said hello but neither of us knew what the other wanted to do or what was acceptable, so the moment became a little awkward for us both, rather than the fantasy reunion I'd imagined. The one thing it highlighted was that we both respected each other and didn't just assume it was okay to hug. I was very aware of letting the boys initiate any kind of physical contact, and I chose the words I was using carefully. I knew I was unlikely to do anything wrong, but there was always the possibility of accidentally saying or doing something that I shouldn't, and this kept me on edge all day. As much as I wanted to, I was unable to relax and enjoy the meeting.

We'd arranged to do various activities on the day. We did crafts together such as making personalised items that we could then take away; swap or Peggy would send on a later date through the letterbox system. We also had lunch and I made decorated buns for us all. Aside from being asked a few questions about my life, the boys spoke to me and acted the way I'd have thought any child would have. RJ became much less reserved as the day went on and we all eventually got our hugs. Though I did relax a little, my anxiety never truly went away, and it put a dampener on the day for me; but seeing the boys happy and healthy was beyond anything I could imagine. I watched the boys play and interact with each other, and with their parents. Overall, it was just a surreal but beautiful thing to be able to witness. I felt incredibly lucky. After saying our goodbyes, Peggy drove me back to the train station and we chatted on the way about how well the day had gone. I spent the train ride home and most of the night talking to Stewart about it. Squealing at just how grown up the boys seemed considering I hadn't seen CJ for five years and it had been four years since last seeing RJ. Even with my nerves, it was a day I knew

I would never forget. The day I got to see both of my sons together, for the very first time. Reunited.

I saw the boys again a couple of days later when Mum and Lisa came with me. Seeing the emotion and the peaceful joy in their faces meant the world to me. As I so often did, I put them first that day and I spent the day a little in the background. I know this wasn't needed but, just as I used to do during contact, I wanted them to have full use of their time with the boys. I took many photos to remember the day. It was like I regressed to the young girl who was so scared of this never happening again, so frightened of time going by that I needed to capture it all. Old habits die hard, obviously. Throughout our day we played, we laughed, we watched home videos of the boys and played some more. We spent the day thoroughly enjoying each other's company to the fullest. CJ and RJ were very bright and witty young boys. Our 'see you soon' really was soon, after all. That day Peggy and Chris gave something back by agreeing to this and we were fully aware of how fortunate we were that they were open to this. Our admiration for them soared over the course of that week.

When our second visit was over, and as we said our 'see you soon', they waved us all off and I could finally be safe in the knowledge that we truly would see them soon. We spent the journey home, much like I did with Stewart on my first day, just talking about how special the boys were and how we'd had such a momentous day with them all. Knowing that for now at least, the pressure was off, I had a cry on the way home as my anxieties were released and I felt able to breathe easy for the first time in a week. There is no sufficient was to describe what it's like to see the children who were taken away from you again. It took me days to process my emotions from it all.

The part of seeing the boys that hit me the most, especially with CJ, was that I thought somehow that meeting them and having that reunion would be like seeing my babies again; having them back in a way. I wasn't too naïve, I understood that they had grown up, still I somehow expected them to be the same in some way. Either by look, or just by the connection just picking up where it left off. When Peggy and I pulled up in the car on the first day and I saw two young boys in front of me, it slapped me right across the face that the little babies I once knew were gone, they stopped existing the moment we said, 'see you soon' and I had to walk away. It was difficult to go into this expecting to find something I felt we had lost, only to realise it was gone forever.

However, the distress of this unexpected revelation was not long lasting once the full effect of the weekend began to wash over me. Watching them all together as a wonderful family unit, they were happy and fit together so perfectly. It was like witnessing four people who were meant to find each other in the world. It felt right. Yet again I was left with a sense of closure that I never knew I needed. Time had helped me heal somewhat, and then meeting Peggy and Chris for the first time I felt it was closure enough to accept what had happened. I wasn't aware that there could be another level of acceptance that would make me look at this differently. I had no idea that after our reunion, I would stop thinking of the boys as mine and instead I would see them as Peggy and Chris' boys, and I was okay with this. After the realisation that the boys I said goodbye to were now gone, but I now had the pleasure of knowing two very different boys, it changed how I saw our meet ups and how I communicated with CJ and RJ. I still got nervous because I knew the boys still had expectations of me and I would always fulfil them to the best of my abilities, but my expectations had melted away with the memory of them as babies. I was finally able to emotionally let go of that part of me and my life.

Chapter Twenty-Three
Life or Death

In August of that year, Stewart and I went on our first holiday together to Disneyland Paris. It is such a magnificent place to go and certainly not just for children, but I can't say I didn't wonder what it would have been like to have had even one of the babies that we lost with us. It made me picture a future version of me and Stewart with a little one, holding both our hands and walking in between us down Disney main street, towards the castle; totally in awe of this magical kingdom. The perfect haven for any family.

Disney had been the basis of all my dreams growing up, it's themes of Prince Charming, happy ever after, and always defeating the baddy were so influential in how I saw the world, so it was always somewhere I'd longed to visit. I'd envisioned it as this fantastical part of the world, and it didn't let me down. We talked about it for weeks after returning, already wanting to go back again. Not long after we did return, Stewart and I suffered our third miscarriage, and I began to think that having a baby wasn't meant for our future. I thought there was something so inherently wrong with my ability to be a mum that even the universe was against me. The amount of times I'd had the carrot of motherhood dangled in front of me, and then I couldn't quite reach out and grasp it, was beginning to eat away at me.

My mental health at the time was already treading water after recently finding out some heart wrenching news about the ill health of a family member. Losing another pregnancy felt like an extra weight trying to push me below the surface, the pain so hard to bear I just tried to ignore it and lock it away in the box in my mind, now full to the brim and struggling to contain it all. I hadn't noticed it had a maximum capacity, and I'd been treating it like a bottomless pit. As this was our third loss I was given the opportunity to have some tests to see if there was a physical reason for the repeated miscarriages. A scan provided a diagnosis of polycystic ovarian syndrome (PCOS). I'd had some of the symptoms such as weight gain, sweating, and severe mood swings. It certainly explained a lot, but unfortunately my doctor informed me that it shouldn't cause miscarriages, in fact it was more likely to cause infertility, so I'd been lucky to get pregnant at all. Nevertheless, he added a note to my file to give me certain meds should I fall pregnant again as a precaution against another miscarriage.

In the latter months of the year, I heard from Peggy to arrange a meet up for next year and we agreed to try and do this annually for as long as the boys wanted. We decided we all enjoyed meeting at the house they rented this year, so they booked the same for next year. It gave us all something to look forward to.

In February 2013, Stewart and I decided that maybe we'd jumped into having such a large house a little too soon as it was starting to feel excessively big. So, we moved to a slightly smaller, cheaper house a few streets away. The amount of time I'd imagined the spare room as a nursery and then had my dream collapse in on itself was too heavy a burden every time I passed the door. We decided not to try for a baby, but also not to prevent it after the news that it may potentially be harder for us to conceive. If it happened, then so be it, and we would cross that bridge when we came to it, but I had lost all hope that it would ever happen for us. In the new house, we decorated to make it our own, we celebrated birthdays and had barbecues, but it wasn't long before we found out we were pregnant again. Apparently, the getting pregnant part wasn't the issue for us at the time, it was staying pregnant that seemed to allude me.

This time, things were very different. With all my pregnancy losses, I hadn't reached the point of hyperemesis starting. This time though, a week after we saw those tell-tale two lines on the test, I was already being sick, much more than I ever had been before. Reluctantly, it made me hopeful that somehow my sickness was a positive indicator. As per my medical notes, I was given meds to try and prevent miscarriage and an early scan to check everything was looking okay. At the scan, there was no heartbeat yet as I was only five weeks, but there were other signs of the pregnancy, so they rescheduled me for another scan in two weeks. It felt a lifetime away. For the first time in any of mine and Stewart's pregnancies I reached the six-week mark. Though I had a huge feeling of relief, it didn't take away the fear of losing the baby. It was only a few days after this that I had my first hospital admission and had to take leave from work. I was given meds and IV fluids and sent home after a week, but I still felt just as sick and nothing I ate or drank would stay down. I was only home two days before I was readmitted. The doctors upped my meds to much stronger ones and I was kept on fluids for much longer. I was already starting to lose weight and I couldn't lay down to sleep at all. I was hardly sleeping and barely functional. I was at a point in the pregnancy where hyperemesis had only just set in when I was pregnant with the boys. It was so much worse than I realised it could ever get.

Over the next few weeks, I wasn't out of hospital for more than two days at any time. My veins were shot from the use of cannulas and blood tests, and there was talk of needing me to go on a feeding tube, such was their concern for my health. I was frail and weak, having lost over a stone and a half in weight within a month. My blood pressure was on the floor, getting lower by the day. I was finding it hard to breathe, with my throat ripped to shreds from all the acid in my vomit. I'd began bringing up blood and my heart was showing signs of great distress. They had tried me on steroids, which is a last resort treatment for hyperemesis, but it seemed to stop all the other meds from having any effect. The IVs couldn't get into my system quick enough to rehydrate me. This was the first time I had ever seen the doctors worried about me before during hyperemesis. Gone was the tutting and the admonishments to just try harder.

I was woken up at 1am by a doctor stopping my fluids and taking urgent bloods. They ran several tests and found that I was in the early stages of acute pulmonary oedema. The next day I spoke to a consultant who said he could give me a feeding tube, but it wasn't guaranteed to stop the vomiting, though I would get more nutrients into my system before it happened. He sat down and in a calm tone told me bluntly that he wanted me to know all the facts about how bad my health was. I was very sick, and there was a very real possibility that if nothing changed both myself and the baby could die. He explained that my heart was struggling, and my body was under immense strain and pressure. He was very clear, and obviously very concerned. I knew what he was telling me. We had a choice to make. We had to decide whether to terminate our baby to save my life.

When Stewart next visited, I asked him to draw the curtains in my cubicle and sit down next to me on the bed. Through tears, I told him what the doctor had said. Stewart sweetly told me that he would be okay if we chose to terminate the pregnancy because he didn't want to risk my life. I knew he hadn't thought about what this meant for us long term, I explained to him that I would give him this chance to walk away guilt free and I wouldn't blame him. Knowing that if we went ahead with a termination, this was it for me. I couldn't face losing another baby, I couldn't have one more goodbye. I couldn't picture a lifetime of adventures with our child just to have it torn from my mind over and over. If we went ahead with the termination, then we would have to move forward in the knowledge that we would never have a child. No other options were available to us. It was a cruel irony that any other woman in this position would have the option of adoption, but not me. This was it for us. So, I gave Stewart the chance to walk away. I asked him to think about it overnight and to let me know his decision the next day. He deserved to be a dad. I couldn't imagine a single man I had ever met in my life who was more worthy of the title, and if I couldn't give him that and if he walked away, then I couldn't hate him for it; I'd let him go. It would be yet another major loss for me.

Sitting in the hospital bed that night, I sobbed, fully aware that there was no easy option for him or me. I was so scared of losing our baby and losing Stewart too. After barely sleeping, I spent the morning sobbing. I didn't want to say goodbye to our much-loved baby. I had tried so hard to get pregnant and I was almost 11 weeks along, but I was also terrified of dying and I couldn't put my family through that. I also had to think of CJ and RJ. I didn't have them in my care, but what would they think if I left myself to die for another baby. Especially after the doctors confirmed that it was highly unlikely that the baby would get to a gestational age when they could survive.

Stewart came to the hospital and I felt the biggest lump in my throat. Time seemingly stopped the second before he opened his mouth to tell me his decision. He chose to stay with me, saying he could have a life without a child, but not without me. In my hormonal, sick and vulnerable state, of course I cried a river. I was so thankful and relieved. We sat and hugged, and I apologised profusely for not being able to carry on with the pregnancy. He understood that I wanted this baby more than anything, but that it wasn't just about what I wanted and there were so many other people to consider in this decision. Mum was beside herself knowing how sick I

135

was, she couldn't get through a visit without crying, though this was to be expected given the seriousness of the situation.

A couple of days later, we said goodbye to our fourth baby. I remained in hospital where my physical health could be monitored until I was well enough to be discharged. However, there was no monitoring of my mental health. I cried into my pillow. Feeling like my heart had been ripped out, knowing it was me who made that choice. The mental anguish was unbearable.

I was discharged the following day. For weeks, I couldn't tolerate being at home because the smells were very triggering for my vomiting. It was bittersweet coming home and being able to relax and sleep in my own bed knowing that I wouldn't have to return to the hospital again and my mood improved.

As if life hadn't dealt us enough of a crappy hand that year, a week later, I held Stewart's hand as he said goodbye to his best friend Havoc. His dog and best friend since Stewart was 16, was now old and frail and unable to walk or even stand. On the vet's advice, Stewart took the decision to let Havoc go peacefully. We were both there with him until he was gone. Before we left, I whispered into Havoc's ear that I would look after Stewart for the rest of my life. This was one of the hardest and most painful things I've ever witnessed, even after what had happened just a week earlier. Seeing the man I loved in so much pain and not being able to make it better for him just broke my heart. On returning home, we fell into each other's arms as soon as we walked through the door; pulled together in our shared grief, we just held each other and let the tears flow.

Chapter Twenty-Four
Love, Life and Loss

In the weeks that followed the hardest month we had ever endured as a couple, we made sure to make time for each other to talk, to cry, and to grieve. This level of loss and grief isn't something that you can easily recover from, and there were days that it felt like it may feel this bad forever. Both of us grieving two very different losses but grieving all the same. We were united in our pain and supporting each other the best we could, and our love grew stronger through the hardship.

We promised ourselves we would live our lives to the full and live it for us. Together we would fill it with laughter and fun, adventures and good times. We had plans of holidays we wanted to go on and New York was at the top of our list. At summer's end, I took self-redundancy from my job after they had to let half of the staff go. It felt like a good time for a new start. I didn't rush into finding another job though, unsure of what I wanted in a career. In the Autumn, we welcomed two new members to the family, a female, all-white, short-haired cat who we named Jess. She was a Daddy's girl from the start and packed a lot of attitude for such a tiny little thing. Stewart, adamant he wasn't a cat person, fell head over heels for her. At night though Jess seemed lonely and cried herself to sleep, so we got her a sibling in the form of Max, an all-black, half-Bengal cat, and they were like yin and yang. Max was a few weeks older than Jess but the complete opposite to her in every way. He was shy and scared of almost everything. He was gentle in nature though with moments of playfulness. The only thing that got him up and moving was food or string. He was quite the gentlemen, and they made the perfect pair.

The time came to see Peggy, Chris, and the boys again. I brought Mum and Lisa again and it was like seeing extended family. We had lunch, played on the scooters outside and my nephew, Jake, came too and he enjoyed playing with his young cousins. I couldn't believe how much the boys had grown in just a year, but they were still the polite, kind, and funny boys we knew from the year before. On the second day, the men folk (as Peggy and I like to say) joined us. My Step-Dad, Lisa's husband, and Stewart all came with us, and I was so excited to see everyone meet. Though my Step-Dad and Lisa's husband never got to say goodbye to RJ, this was special for them after they had been at our 'goodbye' contact with CJ. This was also the first time that CJ and RJ would be meeting Stewart and I was so happy that they were open to this. RJ seemed to take a special shine to Stewart which was lovely to see.

I was reserved about seeing the boys this year, wondering if deciding not to have any children ourselves would make me feel differently. It was a worry leading up to the meet up. Thankfully, I felt the same as I had the year before, which confirmed that I was truly accepting of the situation. I enjoyed seeing the boys with their parents and we were all just as excited to see Peggy and Chris as we were the boys, they were all family to us now. As much as Peggy and I talk over email, it was still nice to have the face-to-face conversations too. As soon as our visit came, it passed just as quickly. We reconfirmed that we felt it would be good to make this an annual get together that the whole family could enjoy. We all said our 'see you soon' and headed home.

The year of 2013 ended with the devastating news that my niece, Rebecca, who was the same age as me, had received a terminal cancer diagnosis. She was the daughter of my half-sister on my Dad's side. My niece and I grew up together and were close when younger, and even though we became distant as we grew, I have so many happy memories of our childhood. We'd still say hello on Facebook, and I would always follow what was going on in her life. Admittedly, I never tried hard enough to keep in touch with many members of my family. With everything that happened with the boys and feeling like I had to hide so much about my life, the fewer people I saw the less fake smiling I felt obliged to do. I know they'd have told me that I didn't have to do that, but I had done it for so long that faking happiness had become second nature. Not feeling I could be open about my feelings made me distance myself from people, especially family. Something I regret every day.

Dad messaged me to say there was nothing more that could be done for Rebecca and I was distraught and after hearing this, I dreamt of her often. Despite not being as close anymore, I was truly devastated, and it affected my mental health so much that I had a break down at work and was dismissed. In April, the day after my birthday, Rebecca married her long-term boyfriend. I was so glad I got to see her that day. She looked stunning in her ivory gown and it was a truly special day for her. She glowed with happiness and I was in awe of her strength. I can only imagine what it was like for her. I wanted to cry the entire time, but I told myself that if she could get through the day, then who was I to cry. This was her day, and I was so grateful and thankful to be a part of it. I soaked in every second I could of my niece that day, knowing it would be the last time I saw her. As we were leaving I looked back at her from across the room and took a moment to silently thank this woman, who was once a best friend to my younger self. I was so proud of her and I wished I'd told her more often.

In July, I heard from Dad that Rebecca wasn't doing well and didn't have long to live. On the 28th of July, I logged on to Facebook in the morning and I saw that a friend had posted a photo of themselves with my niece. I didn't even see their words; I saw the photo and I knew she was gone. Rebecca passed away with her husband and her parents by her side the night before. I let out a deep wailing cry and I slid from my chair and dropped to the floor on my knees. I cried harder than I thought was possible. Even though I knew this was coming, it was somehow still a shock. I was alone so I called Mum and she let me cry hysterically down the phone for a good five minutes. She asked if I wanted her to come over, but I said no. I knew as soon as I'd gotten this initial burst of grief out, I'd be okay. I just needed to let it out. Let it all out.

Chapter Twenty-Five
Tsunami

Rebecca's death released in me a tidal wave of emotion. I had tried to cram too many traumas and too many losses into the box in my mind and now the damn had burst, and I could no longer hold my head above the water. I was drowning.

To create positive change, Stewart and I looked to move again to a bigger house. As we started to look, the house we'd previously lived in came back up for rent and we took our chance. Although we moved out after going through our miscarriages, so much more had happened in our lives since then that it was nice to go back to house that also held many positive memories. We had always loved the house and had made a great connection with the landlord, so we contacted him directly and he agreed to rent to us. He was more than happy to have us move back in, and at the end of August, we moved back, and it was like we had never left.

The year before Peggy contacted me to discuss Matthew, CJ's Dad. He hadn't yet met Peggy and Chris and therefore hadn't had the opportunity to see CJ again. Matthew and I were friends on Facebook, and I had kept him up to date with CJ, but I kept a respectful distance. He then began his own email contact with Peggy and Chris, despite never having met them, though it wasn't as regular as mine. Matthew was in the army at that point and went to Afghanistan. While he was deployed CJ worried about him very much. So, when Matthew returned from active duty, to help smooth the way, I messaged him offering to go to meet Peggy and Chris with him. He agreed and in early July 2014, I jumped on an overnight coach for the eight-hour journey to London where I met up with Matthew.

I hadn't seen him since the care proceedings for CJ. I was nervous to see him, but I was happy for him to finally meet Peggy and Chris. The four of us had dinner together and we chatted, but for the most part I allowed them to get to know Matthew. The evening went well, and Peggy took a photo of me and Matthew together to give to CJ. This was the only photo of us together that he had. I went home on the overnight coach that same night, after spending a few hours catching up with Matthew after our dinner and asking how he felt. We spoke a lot about our past and I apologised for anything I had said about him during the court case. I told him how proud I was of him for following his dreams of being in the army, even if it did worry me on CJ's behalf. Peggy later told me that a few days after our meeting, Matthew and CJ met again and it brought tears to my eyes knowing just how special and important that would have been for them both.

Later in the year we had our annual meet up with the boys, I wasn't my usual self that year though. One of the most complex issues that had sprung from the box and was now floating around in my brain, concerned the loss of CJ and RJ. Since this happened, I hadn't been very natural with children, always feeling like I wasn't supposed to be around them because my own children were taken from me. I felt I had no right to be allowed near any child at all. I had this niggling fear that parents everywhere just automatically knew what had happened and blamed me for it and didn't want me near their kids. Since meeting Stewart, I spent time around his two nieces and nephew and was terrified when they came to visit. I'd over analyse what I should say and do with them. I'd tell myself that it didn't matter because whatever I did it would be wrong. My mind told me that everything I thought I knew about how to be in front of a child, was wrong and would end badly, just like it did with the boys. Surely, if I could do anything right around kids, then mine wouldn't have been taken from me?

These thoughts, along with so many others, were now floating free. Without being locked away they were intrusive and self-sabotaging. During our annual meet up, I allowed my family to be at the forefront and I took a step back both mentally and physically. I did this both because I didn't know how to act in front of the boys anymore, and because I hoped that by putting myself in the background I could hide how much I was struggling mentally. However, the very act of distancing myself made it more noticeable, and afterwards, I received an email from Peggy telling me that CJ had noticed he played with his Auntie Lisa more than he played with me, and he didn't know why. This broke my heart. I never wanted how I felt to negatively affect the boys.

It had been just over a year since Rebecca's death, and with my mental health in decline, I took the decision in mid-2015 to stop working. Getting up every day felt hard, but when I stopped working it made me feel like I had one less burden on my shoulders, and I could focus on getting myself through each day. Self-care became important. I had asked my doctor to put me on a waiting list for therapy, but I knew all too well that these lists were long, and I never seemed to reach the top. In the hopes of giving ourselves something to look forward to, Stewart and I finally booked the holiday we'd always dreamed of and planned a trip New York in January the next year. I was so excited and found it hard to contain myself, even though I repeatedly told myself something bad would happen and we'd never get there. My relentless inner monologue kept reminding me that my dreams never came true, so why should this be any different? The battle to stay positive and keep myself going was hard but doing things that made my heart happy was certainly helping me to get through more days with a genuine smile.

When we had our annual meet up with the boys this year, we switched things up quite a lot. Instead of Peggy and Chris booking the house, they invited us to stay at theirs, in their annex. If you had told me when the boys were adopted that in seven years I would be invited to their house with my partner, I'd have thought it was a joke. Those kinds of things just didn't happen with adoption. I felt unbelievably grateful, not just in being trusted enough to know where they lived, but to stay with them and spend the weekend with them. On the second day, my family came to join us, Peggy and Chris had very generously gifted them a stay at a local hotel the night before so they could come bright and early, and we all had a fantastic time. I did wonder if seeing the house that the boys lived in would be hard, yet another test of just how accepting I was, but it felt like such an insight into their lives that I was just appreciative of being allowed this honour. I knew that this was far from what so many other birth parents are given and at times it could be overwhelming, and I'd often wonder what I did to deserve to be given so much back.

Chapter Twenty-Six
Dreams Come True

The move back to the old house in time for Christmas, along with our impending trip to New York, enabled me to keep my head above water for longer. I felt genuine happiness amidst horrific trauma, each co-existing in my mind, remaining civil for now. After finishing paying for the holiday in November, I knew this meant we were definitely going but I was still scared to get my hopes up. To celebrate Christmas in our new but old house we got a new tree and decorations to make it extra special.

Since our first Christmas together, we kept our Christmas Eve tradition of wearing our Christmas pyjamas, and snuggling up to watch Home Alone together. We placed our seven-foot, artificial Christmas tree on a small table for added height where it could be seen by everyone who walked past our window. The new decorations were all a rich, deep red and alternated with sparkling silver ornaments. We went for traditional looking glass baubles and bows. For the first time ever, we decided not to use tinsel on the tree and instead we had silver beads travelling along the branches. The new lights were a warm white with several functions, we had them on the setting that made them look like twinkling stars. The room was adorned with traditional looking red decorations such as bells, and ornamental Santa figurines. It felt like a grotto, but in a tasteful way. I could have plucked this room from the Christmas dreams of my childhood.

The flickering flames of the fireplace warmed the room up to feel cosy, and the Christmas tree and window lights provided the extra glisten. It was the perfect

Christmas Eve night. The personalised red velvet stockings were hung, and the presents were nestled under our tree, ready for the morning. Our cheese and crackers were laid out on a platter ready for us to snack on during the film. We had showered and were in our red and blue check pyjamas, bought specifically for this night and Christmas morning. I turned to put my phone down and on turning back found Stewart was on one knee in front of me, and in his outstretched hand was a small, black open box with a stunning white gold, halo cut ring.

He nervously asked, "Will you marry me?".

I was so shocked I burst out with, "Oh my god!".

Although I was hopeful he might propose in New York, this was completely unexpected. Yet it was also the perfect moment. Just us, surrounded by the magic of Christmas. It took me a minute or so to realise that I hadn't actually accepted. "Yes!" I blurted out.

We basked in the romance of it all for half an hour and then, wanting to announce it someone, I called my Dad, and he was so happy for us. I couldn't wait to tell everyone else and, although we had gotten people other gifts, this news was going to be my favourite thing to give people this year. After we both got over the shock, and Stewart overcome his nerves, we hugged up close and we watched our film, although I probably spent more time looking at my ring! This was going to be one of those nights that I would remember for the rest of my life.

When Christmas Day came, I was so excited that I couldn't keep it in. Stewart spent the first half of the day with his family, and I came over briefly in the morning with him to tell his mum. She already knew, as she had been keeping the ring, but she hadn't known when it would happen. When Lisa arrived to give me a lift to Mum's for the day, I couldn't help but flash her my hand and we shared a giddy, shrieking moment together before setting off.

When I got to Mum's, I was so inpatient to share the news that I texted Stewart to ask if he minded if I told them before he got there. I suspect he knew I wasn't going to be able to wait all day with my level of excitement. I had opened my Mum and Step-Dad's Christmas card to put an extra note at the bottom before I handed it to them. What had once said just our names, now said 'Love from Laura and Stewart (your future son-in-law) xx'. I wasn't sure if they would get it straight away.

As they read it, I stood by their side, with my hand behind my back and slipped on my ring. They reached the bottom and my Step-Dad laughed, thinking I was probably joking and then he looked at me. Mum started to scream but stopped herself in confusion as to whether what she had read, meant what it said, and then she looked at me too. I threw up my hand with the ring on it and the room burst into screams and yells of congratulations. I knew they would be so happy; I think they'd been waiting and hoping for this for a while too.

That Christmas was so special, but we also had something equally as exciting about to happen in January. As the New Year passed, we started to plan and pack for our trip to New York. The day finally came to set off and I couldn't sleep the night before I was far too excited. We travelled to London on the coach the day before we flew and stayed in a beautiful hotel at Heathrow Airport called the Radisson Blu Edwardian. Waking at 4am, we were on the first hopper bus to the airport, arriving just as all the shops opened, and had breakfast. We'd booked the first flight to New York of the day so that we would get to New York with a good amount of time still left in the day, given the time difference.

Stewart had been to New York twice before. Once with his college as part of his studies, and the second time was in the aftermath of the tragedy of 9/11, when he worked for a disaster recovery company that was hired to help with the clean-up. He lived there for six months and was looking forward to going back and seeing how they had re-built. I knew it would be powerful for him to see New York again, after seeing things first-hand at one of their hardest times. Stewart was also excited to witness me see New York for the first time. Knowing how much of a dream it had been for me to go, knowing how even though I hadn't been before, somehow the city meant so much to me; he was looking forward to seeing my reaction to everything.

One of the first things we did was visit Times Square. Our hotel was in part of Times Square, but not the iconic central part. We were only a couple of blocks away though, so it took us less than ten minutes to get there. We took our first photo together and posted on Facebook to let everyone know we had gotten there safely, and then we called Mum to let her know she could stop worrying. Over the next few days, following Stewart's itinerary to the letter, we saw everything we had wanted to see and went everywhere we wanted to go. At the Statue of Liberty, we went into the pedestal and the view from Liberty Island is breath-taking. It's every photo I've ever seen of New York City, and I was finally there. Lady Liberty is so beautiful and was easily my favourite part of our trip.

It was at the One World Observatory when I realised just how afraid of heights I was, and how thoroughly glad I was when my feet were back on solid ground. While in the area, we visited the 9/11 memorial site and museum. Both me and Stewart had tears in our eyes as we took it all in. It was surreal to see things I'd seen on the TV, in person, and it truly brought home the horror of that day. More so for Stewart having been part of the many teams that helped in the aftermath. It made me feel so proud of him, because it must have been hard, and I can only imagine the things he may have seen.

One of the highlights for me was going to visit Top of the Rock at the Rockefeller Centre. We also visited the Empire State Building. One of the most beautiful moments we experienced was when we visited Central Park. It had snowed prior to us arriving so everything was blanketed in white. I remember walking into the vast openness of the park and suddenly, the city melted away. The exhilarating noise of the New York streets just disappeared, even a minute into the park. As we walked further in, I began to hear jazz music being played by a saxophonist. That moment felt so peaceful, I felt like I was home. In a snowy central park, listening to the saxophone echoing through the tree branches, with Stewart and I walking hand in hand, I felt like I belonged there. It was one of those times where you feel like everything that has happened in your life, had happened exactly right for you to be where you are stood at that exact second, so you can experience this very moment.

This entire trip to New York made me so thankful that I had waited to go. Not that I had ever I had the opportunity to go beforehand, but I'm glad that I never even tried. This way, I got to see it for the first time with my best friend. Ever since then, New York remains our special place, our favourite place on earth. As we sat in the transport bus to the airport and our flight home, we were already talking about when we might return; whenever it was, we hoped it would be soon. We had been bitten by the New York bug. It had been everything I ever thought it was, and much, much more.

Chapter Twenty-Seven
Therapy

After coming back from New York, both Stewart and I hit a downer, something I'm told can be normal after the exciting rush of an engagement or a dream holiday, and we'd recently had both, so it was a double whammy of a downer. For Stewart, that looked like a dose of regular post-holiday blues, but for me it meant sinking deeper into the well of my depression.

As much as the engagement, Christmas and the holiday had been a distraction, all I had in the immediate days ahead was the endless drip of time alone at home. The games my mind played with me were becoming too much to handle. From one moment to the next I had no idea what trauma flashback I would be plunged into: Jason' abuse, the rape, losing my niece, losing the boys. I relived them all. I was overwhelmed. As the weeks and months passed, I managed a brave face but behind it I was emotionally shattered.

I began secretly self-harming again. Something I hadn't done for a long time. When I lived alone after leaving Jason, I was tormented by everything I'd gone through, losing the boys, his control and abuse. I remembered then that, even the shallow scratches that were meant for attention in school had helped to relieve the pain of teenage social isolation. Now, alone and with nobody to stop me, and unable to sleep, I began cutting my thighs; using physical pain to distract from my emotional pain. My cutting didn't need medical attention, but it came close and crossed a bridge, from only ever cutting for attention, to doing it to calm my mental anguish.

I stopped when I met Stewart, because I wanted to be happy again, and happy with him. Now, knowing no other way to ease the torment of my mind, I reached for the knife. I kept the cutting from Stewart because, while I knew he would be supportive, he was my happy place and I needed to keep that happy place unsullied by my past traumas.

I was barely sleeping and crying myself through waves of painful memories I could no longer pretend away. I felt weighed down with stones in my pockets, watching an entire ocean rushing towards me, about to engulf me. Nobody around me recognised how badly I needed help mentally. On the surface, I lived a seemingly normal life but underneath I was paddling wildly. I reached for something to buoy me up and asked Stewart if we could stop preventing pregnancy and see what happened. I confessed I wasn't ready to give up on the idea of being a parent, even while part of me silently recognised this as the bubbling of unresolved feelings. Stewart agreed, and although we weren't throwing everything into getting pregnant, we decided to let nature find its course. We dipped our toes into the water rather than making the commitment of taking a flying leap.

Another life buoy was to begin planning our wedding. We sat down and talked about what we wanted to do; where to get married, who to invite? We created an initial guest and realised it was heavily lopsided because, other than Stewart's immediate family, most of his relatives lived in Scotland. We didn't expect them all to come down for just one day, nor did we expect my family to travel for a wedding in Scotland. Other than family, we didn't have anyone else to invite as we weren't sociable people and didn't have friends. This meant Stewart didn't have anyone for a best man, and I only had Lisa as a potential bridesmaid. We realised an intimate wedding would suit us best. I'm still hazy on who said it first, but we both thought about the same thing at the same time; our ideal wedding was an elopement to

New York! We still wanted Stewart in a suit and tie and me in a proper gown, but we wanted the wedding to be just the two of us, in our special place. We booked it for January 2017, knowing there was a chance we may end up being pregnant when the time came and unable to travel because of my hyperemesis. We had to have hope in our life.

Alongside all this, Stewart had processed enough of his grief over the death of his dog Havoc and was ready to bring another puppy into his life and so we travelled to a farm and met the latest addition to our family. He was the last of a litter of pedigree Labrador pups and only ten weeks old when we brought him home. We gave him the name Axel, he gave us lots of laughter, much joy, and countless sleepless nights. Perfect training for if or when we did fall pregnant.

Meanwhile, in one of our many back-and-forth emails, I mentioned to Peggy that I wasn't coping well, and, with careful questioning, she gently extracted more information from me until I revealed the poor state of my mental health. Peggy offered to help me find someone who could help. Going a step further, she then offered to pay for the therapy that I so desperately needed and finally felt ready to access. I couldn't understand why she would want to help me so much, but I was so appreciative. No more waiting for NHS counselling that may not have worked because of the depth of psychological support I needed. I felt lighter just knowing that I was going to be getting the help and having someone who was willing to get me where I needed to be was incredible. My family would have helped if they could, but I was beyond thankful that Peggy gave me this opportunity. Although I had felt ready to embrace therapy for some time, I remained cautious, believing that it may get worse before it got better, and I put no expectations on myself.

We found a local, private psychotherapist who I started working with on a weekly basis. It was hard at first and the sessions often ended with me crying and feeling much worse. However, being there and talking to someone who could help me to understand my own thoughts and feelings and give me the right tools to help myself when I was at home, was life changing. Going to therapy made me realise that I had already had so many of the inner resources I needed, and that I understood my emotions, my thoughts, and feelings, and how best to respond to them. I worked well with my psychotherapist, and we started doing EMDR therapy too, which works by stimulating one of your senses in order to use them to process the trauma by talking about it as your senses are fired up, this then forges new pathways in your brain that lead to thinking about the trauma in a healthier way. It doesn't work for everyone, but it worked well for me. We took each trauma separately and I processed each one in the session and then I'd go home and write about it all too as this helped me to express what I couldn't voice.

At the beginning of therapy, we created a chronological list of my major life events and my therapist said she had never had a patient face so many significant traumas. At first this upset me and left me feeling bad, because I interpreted it as though I'd done something horrible to deserve it all, and just how rubbish my life must be if I'm the worst she had ever seen. Then I looked at it in a different way. Part of the processing of traumas included visualising a different outcome for the things I'd gone through, a more positive outcome. This was about changing my outlook on those situations and how I perceived them. So, when I heard 'never had a patient face so many significant traumas', I noticed I immediately took this negatively, and thought of myself as being the 'worst' and having a 'rubbish life'. I challenged myself to look at it positively and realised instead that her comment was an acknowledgement of my inner strength, for surviving so many traumatic events. That moment was pivotal for me because it was the point when I knew I could get better.

Therapy was intensive but I felt the benefits after only a few sessions. I began to be able to function better and genuinely enjoy life again. I liked going to therapy, it was like learning to swim again, but I had a lifeguard with me at all times in case a big wave came along to dunk me. It wasn't easy and I would sometimes feel horrible immediately after a session, but I also came out of it feeling productive and eventually felt really good about it. For the first time, I was able to speak to someone in detail about how I felt when I lost CJ. I also shared my lack of connection to RJ, and she helped me to understand that in much more detail than I had before. She noted how so many things were against me from the start in that pregnancy: having lost one child, then falling pregnant so quickly with no space to grieve, Jason' abuse and manipulation, and then RJ taken straight to the NICU without me even seeing him, much less hug him, to kick start the bonding. She also said it was likely that if I never let myself believe he would come home, then I was almost certainly shielding myself from getting hurt again, by rejecting any bond that could have happened to avoid being attached when the inevitable 'goodbye' came.

These were all things that I knew in some small way, but I had no way of knowing if it was just me trying to make excuses to appease my actions, or if they were true acknowledgements of how I was feeling and why. Working with my therapist really catapulted my understanding, and my ability to control my thoughts and feelings. I continued to go even when I was starting to feel much better because I knew therapy for me needed a long-term commitment. I was evermore thankful to Peggy for the opportunity to work through the weight I'd been carrying on my shoulders all this time. I could finally crush that box in my mind; I didn't need it anymore.

Chapter Twenty-Eight
Eloped

In January 2017, Stewart and I once again travelled to New York. The day we got there we headed straight for City Hall to get our marriage licence. Outside the entrance there is a cart run by a gentleman who creates wedding bouquets from fresh flowers, and I ordered one to collect when we returned to get married. I chose a bouquet of roses, with diamantes in the centre of each rose and the centre rose surrounded by gypsophila. I loved my bouquet and wished I could have brought it home with me.

Our second day we went to Liberty Island to see the beautiful Statue of Liberty again. It was a freezing cold day, minus nine degrees, with strong winds and news of a storm about to hit the island. We went back to the hotel and only ventured out again that day for food. On the eve of our big day, we ate at our favourite restaurant, John's Pizzeria, which seemed apt as it's in an old church building. It doesn't look like much from the outside but when inside it has high ceilings with an intricate stain glassed roof and a large, detailed mural on the main wall. It has seating on the ground floor and then an upstairs mezzanine that runs along the wall so you can overlook the entire restaurant. It was the perfect night for both of us.

Back at the hotel, I gave Stewart his wedding gift from me. I didn't want him to cry on the day, and I suspected he might, so I gave it to him early. I had bought him a pair of cufflinks to wear on the day that included a photo of Havoc. Along with the cufflinks, I gave him a short poem I had written:

To My Handsome,

I couldn't let you get married without your best friend…

There is a role inside your heart that I will never try to take.

There is a bond between you both that will not ever break.

There is a little sorrow now because he isn't near.

But I couldn't let you get married without your best friend being here.

I love you with all my Blue Heart.

xx

'With all my Blue Heart', is our special sign-off for each other. Close to the start of our relationship Stewart sent me a text message with a blue heart on the end. I thought this meant he was feeling sad, but he explained that he thought blue hearts were less commercial, and since then it's been our own little symbol. Stewart did well not to cry when reading the poem, but I think we were both very tired and nervous about the big day. I expected to struggle with sleep but travelling, and being away from home, helped me to fall asleep quickly. At 4am, I woke and peeked outside, to find it had started snowing and there was already a blanket of white on the ground. I didn't expect to get back to sleep for worrying the snow might become so bad that we had to call off the wedding, but as I lay in bed with the TV on quiet, I eventually drifted off.

When we woke on the morning of the wedding, the first thing I did was look outside. The sun was beaming down and there was a fresh layer of snow on the ground. We couldn't have asked for anything better for a New York winter wedding. We had arranged for breakfast in bed, not something we usually do when we are away but neither of us wanted to venture outside and it was our big day after all. I had booked someone to come and do my hair and makeup, something I knew was a risk without having a trial first. She was aware that we needed to be out of the door by 10:15am and it was 9:00am when she arrived. Stewart got ready in the living area while we were in the bathroom and when he was done, he went down to the lobby to wait for me so we didn't initially see each other, and we would get a 'first look' in the lobby instead.

By 9:45am the makeup artist was only just getting to my hair and it became obvious I had made a mistake. I didn't like how she had done my makeup, and because of this I didn't trust to ask her to re-do it, not that we had the time. When she started doing my hair it was clear she hadn't done it before as she wasn't sure what to do and didn't do it well at all. She seemed very nervous, maybe because we were pressed for time. She had amazing reviews and photos of her with other brides that had reviewed her saying she did fantastic. I wondered if the fact that we didn't have a trial, put her on the spot and it just didn't work out. I paid her and she left at the time that I should have been downstairs meeting up with Stewart. Instead, I was having a meltdown in the hotel bathroom. I wiped off what she had done, and I quickly did my makeup myself. I was in no way experienced, but I was thankful that in my time off work, one of things I had chosen to do was to learn to do my own makeup better, and I had invested in some decent products that were more suited to my skin tone. I managed to do something quickly that I was relatively happy with, especially compared to how I looked before.

My dress was an A-Line style, champagne coloured with a white lace overlay. It had a sweetheart neckline with a fitted waist, and it flowed out from there. Despite having had it fitted, it felt snug, but I managed to get it done up by myself. With it being cold, I was particularly thankful that I had thought ahead to bring a white cotton cardigan to put on and it went surprisingly well with the dress. I had re-done my hair putting it half up and half down with slight curls. I rushed down to the lobby and could see Stewart sat with his back to me. I tapped him on the shoulder, and he turned around. This was the first time I had ever seen Stewart in a suit, and the first suit that Stewart had ever worn. He looked so handsome. He wore a black traditional tux but had a straight black tie instead of a bow tie. I had a little cry but told myself to snap out of it, we didn't have the time and I didn't want to cry all my makeup off.

We went down to the entrance to the hotel and asked for a taxi, this would be our first ride in a yellow cab. As it pulled up, Stewart lifted the back of my dress and as I leant to get in the car I both heard and felt an almighty rip at the back of my dress. The zip had popped open and broken off. I was in complete hysterics at this point, wondering why we'd thought we should get married without our family, on our own, somewhere we didn't know and without any planning. I was beside myself over the smallest things. As luck would have it, I had buttons all down my dress that I hadn't been able to do up myself, and so in the back of the cab, on the way to City Hall, already late and trying to contact our photographer to let her know we were on our way, Stewart did up all the little buttons on the back of my dress. It did the trick and held the dress, but I can tell in the photos that the dress wasn't fitting me properly.

In one last attempt for this day to break me completely, once we had fixed the dress issue, I realised that in my efforts to rush down to Stewart, I had forgotten to pick up the rings! That was it, I was crying again. When we arrived, our photographer met us at the car and told me to stop crying, the guy who sold the flowers also did cheap rings for this very reason. As many times as things went wrong, luck remained on our side. We used my engagement ring as my wedding ring and bought Stewart

158

a simple silver band that wasn't too dissimilar from the one sat in our hotel room. We picked up my flowers and Stewart's buttonhole, a simple red rose, on the way inside and I calmed myself down in preparation to marry the man I loved.

The photographer was so sweet and had us laughing within minutes. There were many other couples waiting inside because all you have to do is present your licence and fill out a form, take a ticket and wait for your number to be called. It was such an amazing atmosphere, to sit and watch all the other couples coming in and out, and ogle at everyone's chosen outfits and play a bit part in their special day. It all felt incredibly magical.

When our number was called, I Facetimed Mum and John so they could watch the ceremony, placing my phone of the pedestal the officiant was using, so they were there with us. Stewart and I held hands and repeated the words of the short, non-religious ceremony and it was perfect. I tried to hold back the tears long enough to get the words out. I had longed for this day since the moment I met Stewart. We had been through so much together, and I was thankful that after everything he still chose me. He truly was my absolute best friend, my happy place and I couldn't have imagined a better way to marry him, than in the place that meant the most to us in this world. The day didn't exactly go to plan, but I knew at the end of the day being able to call Stewart my husband made it all so worth it, and what a story we'd be able to tell everyone!

Chapter Twenty-Nine
Trying

In mid-2017 it was almost a year since we had decided to 'stop preventing' pregnancy and we hadn't yet gotten pregnant. We decided it was time to book an appointment with a specialist, given how easily we had gotten pregnant before. Being in a much better place mentally, and still seeing my therapist, I wanted to talk to someone about putting a medical plan in place to both prevent a miscarriage and have in place a thorough treatment plan for the hyperemesis. If we were going to continue trying for a baby, we may as well do everything we could. I was referred and it wasn't long before I saw a consultant.

To help prevent miscarriage the consultant simply put in my notes to use the same drug I was given the last time, as it seemed to work. We then spoke about my hyperemesis, which this consultant was well informed about. She spent time looking over my medical history and decided that if I got pregnant we would skip any medications that had never previously worked and requested in my notes that I should be started on a much stronger drug. Also, I was told I could self-admit to the hospital by coming straight in, instead of going through my doctor, which had often been a stumbling block. Feeling confident that we had a great plan, she gave us advice for other things we could try to get pregnant. We shifted from 'not preventing' to actively trying to get pregnant. We were doing ovulation tests, tracking my cycles, the whole shebang.

When nothing was happening, we just kept going and in the meantime, we got on with our lives. We hoped that at some point we would see two lines on a test, but it was harder each month that went past to see a negative result and I began to resent those around me who were pregnant. I started a new job but on realising there was a pregnant woman working there I had to leave. I decided it was best for me not to be faced with something that I was struggling with daily if I wasn't strong enough to look past it. I almost told Stewart I wanted to stop trying, but I knew I wanted this so badly that the mental torture of not getting pregnant was worth it for the hope that one day we would be. I knew I could quit now, be upset and I'd be guaranteed to never be a mum. Or I could carry on, still be upset but have hope that at least we still had that chance of seeing our baby one day.

Peggy and I arranged the years meet up, and adjusting to the boys getting older, she felt it would be better to go somewhere different and make it a one-day event, which we agreed felt like the right thing to do. We chose to spend the day at Newby Hall, somewhere I had never been, and we arranged it for August, it was a beautiful sunny day. The inside of the hall was closed for a private event, so we mostly walked around the grounds and enjoyed the outdoor areas. It was such a picturesque venue with a small river for paddling boats and a play area around the edge, there was even a little train that you go on and a ride through some of the grounds. Perfect for growing and lively boys. As we left, we went through the gift shop and Stewart bought an elephant soft toy, not for himself or me, but for the baby he said he knew we would have one day. This just about melted my heart, and we treasured that little elephant, although we put off naming him until he had an owner.

A whole year passed, and nothing had changed. We still hadn't gotten pregnant, and we needed to take our minds off that cold, hard fact. Fulfilling our promise to ourselves we booked to go to New York, only this time we went for a couple of days in the summer of 2018. We visited the amazing Coney Island which we loved, it was 32 degrees and perfect blue skies. This area felt more like Los Angeles than New York, especially in the hot weather. The heat rises from the concrete in the city and as the breeze whistles through the buildings, its humidity hits you in the face. We explored Brooklyn and finally managed a walk across Brooklyn Bridge. After two previous visits, we finally got to see Central Park in full bloom, and we had the most serene bike ride along the coast. Even though we weren't there for long, we crammed more into those days because the weather was so good and seeing fresh parts of the city felt like we'd had an entirely different holiday than our first two experiences. When we got back we continued trying for a baby and a few months later I ended up having emergency surgery to remove my appendix. This meant having to take a break for a while until I was fully recovered. It felt like the world just didn't want me to have a baby.

Peggy and I had been talking a lot more over email lately, we'd be discussing our story about how we came from no contact to seeing each other annually with my whole family. We realised we worked well together in trying to arrange our yearly meet ups and we both wanted to share our story of adoption, in the hopes of showing people that contact after adoption could be done differently to just writing an annual letter. We were both big advocates for it, given it was going so well for us. After many emails back and forth, we agreed to create a podcast together, initially to share our story, and then see where we wanted to go afterwards. We planned on starting after Christmas, in January 2019. I told Stewart that if we weren't pregnant by the end of the year then I wanted to stop trying, at least for a little while so I could do the podcast with Peggy. It was getting too hard to constantly see the negative tests when we were doing everything in our power to get pregnant. The podcast gave me something creative to focus on.

December came and it was our final month of trying for a baby. One day, while Stewart was at work, I fell down the stairs at home and, although I was lucky not to be seriously injured, I was in a lot of pain in the coccyx area. I went to A&E, but they said they don't scan for coccyx breaks because there is nothing they can do to treat it. If it was broken then it could take months to recover but if it were simply badly bruised, then it may take a few weeks. I was gutted that we had been robbed of our last month of trying for a baby. I took it as a sign that we should just give up. A week later, the pain was improving so it looked likely to be a simple bruise. Out of habit I had still been taking my ovulation tests and I got a positive. Usually this would mean we would need to start trying but we couldn't because of my injury. The next night I panicked about giving up on our last month and I said I wanted to try and if it hurt then we could just stop. We tried once and it hurt more than I had thought it would, so we didn't do it again. I told myself we would just start trying again next year, after the podcast was completed. Peggy and I were excited about the podcast and, with the planning done, we were ready to begin recording after Christmas. But then came an unexpected delay.

Chapter Thirty

Our Fight

On the 30th of December 2018, I was so impatient I took a pregnancy test. We'd only tried once since I'd fallen down the stairs and was badly injured, and yet my brain urged me to take a test. I was due my period any day and had been feeling the signs that it was on its way, and yet my brain insisted I take a test. I took the test and barely checked the result because I was so sure it would be negative, yet two lines told another story.

To prevent me from getting my hopes up I asked Stewart to run down to the local shop and get another test. Only a cheap one though because I still felt there was no point in getting an expensive one, and even if I did it was unlikely to show anything this early. He returned with a pack of two tests, and I took one. I still wasn't convinced when I saw the faintest of lines, so I took the other one which I also saw two lines on. I allowed myself to get a little excited, but Stewart wanted me to do a digital test, one that showed the word 'pregnant', rather than relying on two lines. The problem was that there hadn't been any digital pregnancy tests in stock at the shop. I rang Mum and she arrived with a Clearblue pack, which includes a criss-cross test and a digital test. I did the criss-cross one first. The tally was now four positive tests. I took the digital test and the words 'Pregnant 1-2 weeks' showed on the screen.

Risking another fall, I practically bolted down the stairs screaming that I was pregnant to Stewart and I ran in to his arms. My Mum and Step-Dad had retreated to their car across the street, and so I opened the door and shouted to them across the road, jumping up and down in the doorway before bursting into tears. For the first time in a long time, I cried happy tears. Not one to wait, I grabbed the 'I heart NY' baby vest we purchased in New York, and placed it with the digital test, and took a photo to use for our announcement. I knew we could miscarry, but I always liked to announce our pregnancies because even if we lost the baby, they still existed, and I didn't want to feel like I had to hide that they were ever here. I posted it to Facebook that day, after we made sure to tell Stewart's family, and everyone was over the moon for us.

As soon as I could call them in the New Year, I spoke to the doctors and got the medication I needed to prevent a miscarriage and what I needed to take as soon as the hyperemesis started. Although, it was worrying that I didn't need them yet. In our fifth week, I had a bleed, and we assumed the worst. I was sent for a scan which showed a gestational sac but nothing else at the time. I was asked to come back in a few weeks. I kept on taking my medication, and kept on taking pregnancy tests, which kept on insisting I was pregnant. I was given a blood test to check if my HCG levels were good and rising and they were but not fantastically well. The bleeding kept stopping and starting and at our next scan they saw the gestational sac and the yolk sac but again nothing else. At the time, we would have been seven weeks along and should have been able to see something by now. The staff kept telling me it may just be too early, but knowing me and Stewart had only tried once, I knew the dates were more and more unlikely for a viable pregnancy.

I started to bleed very heavily after that and having been there before I knew what had happened. I broke the news that we had miscarried again. I was beyond heartbroken. I didn't know if I was strong enough to do this again. I knew I wasn't strong enough to lose another child. In the following weeks, the bleeding continued, and I began feeling sick. I wasn't being sick, but I felt like I was dying.

I was invited in for another scan because they were concerned that I may have a retained pregnancy, or I could be getting an infection. I lay on the bed with the tissue over me and they did an internal scan to make sure they got a clear picture of what was going on. There was total silence. Then the sonographer turned to me and said, "Well someone's still at home and has a heartbeat". I nearly fell clean off the bed with shock and began crying.

I had had a little niggle that told me this sickness might be the start of hyperemesis, and I might still be pregnant, but my mind told me I was trying to deny yet another loss because it was too painful. I thought it was too much to hope that this little, tiny part of me that still had faith, would be right. They measured me at seven weeks, which still confused me, but I was far too happy to argue the dates and I just went with it. Riding on a cloud sheer exhilaration.

I had another scan booked in for two weeks' time and Mum and Stewart came. Still with a heartbeat, they got to see our little one wriggling around and it looked like a little bean. They were still in there, safe and growing and after that I started to worry a little less about the bleeding. They couldn't find a reason for it, which in some ways was good because it meant there was nothing that was obviously going wrong at least. That same week I was admitted to hospital for the first time with hyperemesis. It had arrived with a vengeance and I was unable to take in any food or drink and was becoming too dehydrated, so was admitted for fluids.

I had called Social Services as soon as I could in January, and again when we found out that I was still pregnant. I didn't want to be seen to be hiding this from them, and I wanted to do everything that I was meant to do. I wanted them to come and see us as soon as possible, but I tried not to make Social Services the focus of the pregnancy. At twelve weeks, I felt like I could breathe a little easier even though the bleeding continued, I knew that the statistics for miscarriage fell after this point. Though I'd had so many losses that the fear never truly went away.

Back in 2008, I started a support group for women with hyperemesis. It was the first of its kind and although it was not the biggest group now, I still took a lot of pride in the support we had offered each other over the years. I had announced my pregnancy to the group and had been using it for my own support when a BBC journalist reached out and asked if I wanted to be part of the piece they were putting together for the International Hyperemesis Gravidarum Awareness Day on May 15th. I am a huge advocate for people everywhere who suffer from hyperemesis so of course, I agreed. I was asked to start making a video diary of my days and experiences, no matter how bad, so long as I felt comfortable doing so. I had already been doing this a little myself for my own records, so each week I sent across any videos I'd recorded for editing later, to form part of their news broadcast in May. Some people asked how I managed to film my days and I told them, if sharing my darkest days with hyperemesis helps someone else going through it, then it will have been worth it.

At 16 weeks, we had a private scan to find out the gender of our baby. It took some juggling and jumping around but they finally started to cooperate, and we found out we were having a girl! I was so incredibly happy, I would have been either way, but knowing this would be our only baby I had quite wanted a girl. We already had her name lovingly picked out. That same week, I was thankful that the bleeding finally stopped. We never found a reason, but I was much less stressed once it finally stopped.

As I continued the videos for the BBC, at 18 weeks, I had my final visit to the hospital. The hyperemesis was still there, but due to the great management of my medication this time around, I no longer needed regular IV fluids and I managed at home from that point. In the same week, we met the social worker who had been assigned to us. We showed her our home and she asked us questions about our life, job, family, and everything else imaginable. We were happy to give her any and all information she needed. I told her I was an open book and if she had any other questions, she need only ask. I wanted to be fully cooperative. I explained that if they wanted me to do any assessments to ensure we could bring our daughter home, they should get them done quickly because my consultant had confirmed our baby was likely to arrive early.

We saw our social worker, Kate, only a few times although we did have a few phone calls too, and every time I stressed to her that if they needed a psych report, then they needed to get it done as soon as possible. Kate said she didn't think anything was needed and planned to recommend they simply visit a few times once our baby was home. While I was happy with her recommendation, I was also sceptical that the Panel would accept this without a psych assessment.

Sure enough, the Panel needed me to have a mental health assessment, to be completed by a private psychologist of their choosing. The stress of them taking their time, coupled with the need to have an assessment, was getting to me, and making my hyperemesis worse again. Overall, I wasn't doing well. Stewart had been a great support throughout the pregnancy, always bringing me anything I wanted as I was mostly still bed bound. He'd fetch me drinks and food and keep me company.

If I hadn't had enough things thrown at me during the pregnancy, we also found out I had a short cervix. This meant that there is a high risk of losing the baby, especially before the age of viability. When this happens, they do a procedure where they put a stitch in the cervix to help keep the baby in. However, the procedure itself carries a risk of miscarriage. I truly thought this was it, this was how this dream was going to end. I was so used to good things going badly that I went home and told myself to prepare for another loss. Just as I was starting to believe that this truly could happen for us. I was beside myself with the choice we were faced with. Do nothing and possibly miscarry, do the procedure, and possibly miscarry. I was given a week to decide and put on progesterone pessaries to see if this would make any difference.

With what felt like an angel watching over us, when we went back the week after, my cervical length had improved. The doctors couldn't explain it, they said this wasn't meant to happen and the medication they'd given me was only to try and stop it from getting worse, it wasn't meant to make the cervix long again. In the following weeks, my cervix continued growing until reaching a length that was considered normal. It was a miracle. My body was fighting for this baby. With our history of miscarriage, and everything I'd gone through with the boys I was struggling to allow myself to feel hopeful that this time I would bring a baby home to stay. It felt like such a huge thing to hope for, and I knew all too well the pain I would feel if it all went wrong. So, while I outwardly seemed okay, inside I was always prepared for the worst, never allowing myself to get too complacent, too happy for the future I wanted so badly. In an effort to keep our spirits up, Stewart started to decorate the spare room to begin turning it into the nursery that we had so lovingly planned out for our longed-for little girl. We went with a light blue colour, with soft cream carpets and white furniture. The room wasn't overly big, so we wanted to keep it light and airy. One night when we were adding the final touched to the room, before the cot arrived, Stewart was setting up the baby monitor. It had a night light; a star light show that shone stars onto the ceiling and lullaby music. We closed the curtains to try it out and as the music played and the light show beamed across the ceiling, I burst into tears. It was the first time I'd ever had a nursery, and for a split second

I let myself think about bringing our little girl home to this room, and into our arms. The pain of the fear I felt from one single moments hope and happiness was overwhelming. My past trauma had taken away my ability to allow myself even a second of positivity in this pregnancy.

In early May, with my feeling well enough to withstand meeting up with minimal movement, Peggy and I arranged our annual get together. We both felt it was important for the boys to see me while pregnant, so they could see I was okay and doing much better. We chose to go for a meal local to us to minimise my travelling, and along with my family, we had lunch together and then hung out in a big park across the road. We sat on a bench chatting as the boys, large and small, played with their remote-controlled cars. It was a stunning day with crystal clear blue skies. Physically, I couldn't do much, but it was still good to see everyone, albeit briefly compared to our normal meet ups. However, we knew that we would see them again once our little one was born, so the boys could meet their little sister.

On May 15th, my hyperemesis video was shown nationwide on the BBC, and on their website and social media pages. People messaged me left, right and centre with words of support, and to say how much the video made them feel less alone with their own experience of suffering with hyperemesis. I was so humbled by the comments from people, and so proud of myself for being a part of this.

The pregnancy was now happily moving along, and Social Services got back in touch to say they wanted me to have my psych assessment soon. They told me where it was but that I had to plan how to get there, and they would reimburse the costs. The psychologist was based in Huddersfield and unable to come to me. At the time, they wanted me to travel, I would have reached the point in my pregnancy where I could give birth at any time; past 30 weeks. I couldn't take anyone with me, although they could come and wait in the waiting room, but they'd have to pay for themselves to get there if I did that. I had two appointments, so I'd have had to do it twice. I wasn't familiar with Huddersfield and felt it was wrong to expect me to travel on public transport in my condition, especially as they could have arranged this for weeks ago. I wasn't happy and as a compromise they arranged for a taxi to take me and bring me back but before this could happen my waters broke.

We headed to the labour ward, fearing the worst, because I was still only 30 weeks and five days. I'd been given the steroid injections already, but was still scared because I knew that, just because everything turned out okay with CJ and RJ when they were born early, it didn't mean it would this time. I was kept in and monitored closely, everyone fully expecting me to go into labour that night. Yet it was not until around 9pm the next night that I started to feel little twinges and I knew, in a matter of possibly hours, we would meet our daughter, and we would finally have what we had fought so hard for. A family.

Chapter Thirty-One
My Fight

When Stewart got to the hospital, I was already feeling the contractions slightly stronger, but he was still able to get me through them laughing and smiling so I knew it could be a while yet. The tightening's stayed at this level for a while and then gradually I couldn't get through them without grunting or quietly letting out a yell here and there. They knew that when labour started, they needed to put a cannula in my arm for a drip that could help prevent certain injuries in the baby. I'd been told about this when I was admitted on the Friday and the nurse had explained it all to me and Stewart, the drip would last only a short time, but given my labours were quick it needed to be given as soon as possible so I could have as much of the IV as possible before the baby was born.

The nurse had told me it could be a pretty trippy drug to have, saying that some ladies describe it as 'impending doom', it's not an exaggeration to say that I had been worrying myself sick about this drip since she told me that. Not something an anxious person wants to hear, and I wondered why a nurse thought it was appropriate to use that terminology with someone. However, I didn't much care once I was in labour, I just wanted them to get things moving quickly to help our little girl, and so they came to try and fit the cannula.

I don't have good veins at the best of times, but when I'm pregnant with hyperemesis, they seem to disappear altogether. The first doctor struggled and ended up blowing a vein quite badly in my wrist, but luckily, when they tried it again, they managed to get it in. Once the scary needle part was over I realised that the contractions were hurting much more than I had noticed. I started using gas and air as the pain of this labour seemed different; I was feeling everything in the back, I'd never had that before, and it was much more intense than I remembered.

After what seemed like a very long wait, a doctor finally came to do a check on far along I was. As this was my third labour, from the pain I guessed I was around 4-5cm dilated but the doctor said my cervix was long and closed, which indicated that I wasn't even in labour. I was incredibly confused, but they attributed the pain to a urinary tract infection (UTI), without even checking that I had one. I later found out that I didn't have a UTI at all.

The pain continued to get worse, but the midwives kept telling me I wasn't in labour and I had a UTI. I was hysterical with the pain and was terrified. I was screaming for someone to believe me and to help me. I heard a woman in another room screaming during her labour, I said to them "She's screaming because she's in labour, why am I screaming? This isn't normal for a UTI". It occurred to me that my notes stated I had a past with mental health issues, and I wondered if the staff were ignoring me, thinking I was having a psychotic episode. Although I'd never been psychotic, I wondered if they saw 'mental health issues' on my notes and decided for themselves what that meant. I was an adult woman in her third labour, yet was being condescended to and dismissed, surely there had to be an explanation for their behaviour. Nobody would listen when I repeatedly told them that I was in labour.

Instead, they continued standing at the end of my bed with their arms crossed while I begged them to check my cervix again. They refused and one even snapped at me, shouting sarcastically, "What would you like us to do?" It was clear they didn't believe me. I began going back and forth to the toilet almost every 30 seconds, something I'm sure made them think they were right. On one visit, I realised that it was blood I was discharging and not urine. Yet when I told them it still made no difference, and they stubbornly refused to check my cervix.

Suddenly, I felt an urge to push and because no doctor or midwife was listening to me, I started to panic. I was yelling that I needed to push, but I didn't know whether I should, considering the midwives were saying I wasn't even in labour. I was beginning to doubt myself and started questioning whether it was labour or not. I was more scared than I had ever been, and terrified that I was dying, if this pain wasn't labour then I thought it meant something was going very wrong. In that moment, I cried out for Mum. I knew if she was here, she'd be on my side. Stewart had been fantastic, telling me to breathe and reminding me to use the gas and air, but he wasn't a woman, he had no idea what labour looked like for me, but Mum did and for a second I wished I'd had her there with me too.

At the end of the bed, I heard the same sarcastic midwife say, begrudgingly, "we'll have to check her again she's adamant she's in labour". The attitude made me feel like I was completely alone in that room despite it being full of people. She put on her gloves and got down on the bed but before she even touched me she shouted, "She's crowning", and the entire staff burst into action and came rushing into the room. Honestly, even with the pain, I was so relieved at that moment that I knew my own body and had known I was in labour. Machines were brought in and suddenly there were so many people surrounding me, which was overwhelming. I wanted to question whether it was entirely necessary for them all to be in there, but I had work to do and so did they. In a few short pushes our little girl arrived. They lifted her up so I could briefly see her, which meant more to me than they will ever know.

After my experience with RJ, seeing her before she was whisked away was such a small but incredibly meaningful gesture.

As they were cleaning her, checking over her and doing what they needed to do, Stewart went over to take her first photo and to say hello. I delivered the placenta quickly and was cleaned up by the midwives. I was sobbing from the shock of what had just happened. The labour was officially recorded in my medical notes as just four minutes. Official records in official files. I knew differently.

Exhausted from the trauma of the labour, all of it, not just the final four minutes, meant I struggled to even process what just happened beyond an awareness that it wasn't the labour I had hoped it would be for my last child. The lack of support from the staff, and their hostility, had taken that from me. One of the kinder midwives was gracious enough to apologise for not believing me, which made all the difference. But she was one among many.

They seemed to clear the room as fast as they had entered it, leaving Stewart and I alone. Eventually, two doctors came in to say that our daughter was now in the NICU and doing well. She had breathing assistance in the form of a mask, but provided everything continued to go well, she would likely come off it within 24 hours. They said we could go up shortly, once we were ready. It had been a long night and by the time we even thought about sleep it was already getting light outside. I sent a quick message to all my immediate family telling them the news, but asking them not to tell anyone for now, I just wanted them to have something to wake up to. Mum, who had probably not slept waiting for that text, messaged back to say 'congratulations, you did it, I love you'. I very much needed that message.

We decided it would be best for Stewart to go home, get some rest and see to the animals before seeing our little girl. I knew he would want to be less tired and feel his best when meeting her properly for the first time, but he was happy for me to visit her. I tried to get some sleep while waiting for someone to come and take me to her. I was surprisingly restless; so eager to see my baby. As I was wheeled into the room, she was laying on a hot pink fleece blanket with white hearts on it. She was wearing a tiny nappy and a breathing mask. She had quite a bit of hair over her body as she was so early, and her skin was dark and orange from jaundice, which is common in premature babies. With tubes going in and out of her, and machines bleeping, I was transported back in time, to when RJ was born, and he was laying in the exact same room.

I sat down by the side of her incubator and I watched her for over an hour and before I left, I placed the elephant Stewart bought at Newby Hall in the incubator to keep her company. We named him Ralph. I couldn't believe that I'd gotten through it all. After fighting so hard to get pregnant, to stay pregnant and then with such a traumatic labour, she was finally here; and she was worth every second of heartache.

Ava Rebecca Ivy Anderson was born at 2:09am, weighing just 3lbs 9ozs. She came into the world on the 14th of July 2019 and made a family complete.

Chapter Thirty-Two

Her Fight - Part One

Stewart came back to the hospital with Mum and John after having some much-needed sleep and a shower. We all went to see Ava in the NICU, and I watched as Stewart laid eyes on his daughter properly for the first time. Stewart isn't an overly emotional type, though I was surprised when I looked over to him just after Ava was born and saw that he had a few tears. It made the moment so special. The biggest moment would come when he would be able to hold her.

Over the course of Ava's first day, most of her grandparents came to meet her, along with her aunt and uncle. Those that didn't make it on the first day, quickly followed over the next few days. Ava came off breathing assistance after the first day, which was a great start. Being on the NICU, for a baby born as early as Ava is not a quick thing. Slow and steady wins the race in cases like Ava's, and we knew she would be there for some time and expected to spend the next couple of months going back and forth daily. We also knew that information about how well she was doing wouldn't come for some time. For now, we just had to wait and see what happened, but there were no immediate concerns.

I contacted our social worker to let her know that Ava had been born and that things would now need to be moved along quickly. Even though we had a bit of time, I didn't want to get to the point of Ava being able to come home in a few months and still not have an answer from Social Services as to whether she was allowed home with us. I had to wait a couple more weeks for the psychology assessment knowing nothing would happen until after both appointments and the report had been written. In the meantime, I kept Kate updated on Ava's progress.

In Ava's first week she was given a routine scan that is given to all babies that are born under a certain gestation. They assured us it was nothing to worry about and it was done as standard, and they had no concerns at the time about how she was doing. But the next day, when I came to see Ava in the morning while Stewart was at work, the doctor wanted a quick talk with me. I felt a lump in my throat straight away, but I didn't initially relate it to the scan results. They took me to what looked like an office that was doubling as a storeroom. There was a big window, yet the room seemed dark. I was sat on a dusty smelling sofa and the room felt cold despite it being the middle of July, and warm outside. The doctor sat in the desk chair to my right, with the nurse sat directly opposite me. Two people in a dark, uninviting room, sitting in front of a girl at one of the hardest times of her life. I had been here before. This moment certainly echoed that Social Services office when my life fell to pieces. I could hear my heartbeat thumping in my head.

Ava had a severe bleed on the brain. It was an intraventricular haemorrhage bleed (IVH). They were graded in severity and Ava's was diagnosed as Grade 4, the most severe, which meant that the bleeding was occurring in the brain tissues around the ventricles. They couldn't say why this had happened, though we knew from my regular scans that she didn't have this before she was born. The doctor told me it can be a high risk with babies as premature as Ava. Sadly, there was nothing that could be done, and we simply had to wait for the bleed to stop and when it did they would have more of an idea of the damage it had caused. Though most of any damage may not become apparent until Ava started to grow and develop, they said a common side effect of this type of bleed was Cerebral Palsy, the severity of which would depend on the amount of damage from the bleed; a bleed already graded as the most severe, and one that was still developing. Although the bleed was not currently life threatening, in some cases, it can be.

In the space of a 15-minute chat, I'd been told more medical information than I'd heard in my entire 31 years on this planet. I couldn't hold back the tears and it was like I'd been floating on a cloud that suddenly evaporated and dropped me like a stone into the cold, dark sea. The doctor and nurse gave me time alone to collect my thoughts and pick myself up off the floor, although not literally because somehow I'd remained upright. I wanted to stay in that room forever and pretend that my daughter wasn't suffering in an incubator across the hall. I wanted to go back to having her inside me where she was safe and protected from this world that only ever seemed to show me cruelty. I walked slowly into Ava's room and, as I reached her bedside, I collapsed in tears in the chair.

I stayed for a while just staring at how beautiful and perfect she was, but I knew I needed to start telling people. I went home when I knew Stewart would be home for dinner. He walked through the door, and I immediately reassured him that Ava was fine, but went on to say that I had some news, and he should sit down. This wasn't something a wife should have to tell her husband. I told him as much as I could remember and we both sat and cried in each other's arms. He took the afternoon off work and we went to the hospital straight away, so that the doctors could talk to him and fill in any of the blanks I was sure I'd left, and he could see Ava and hold her little hand.

Slowly, we told each member of our family and, since Ava was so loved by so many who had been following my entire pregnancy journey on my Facebook page, later that day I posted to let people know what was going on. Our family were understandably very upset, and Mum called me several times that day for me to explain what was wrong with her so she could process it in her mind. Stewart and I cried, probably more than we ever had before and we were heartbroken for Ava and the future we now imagined for her.

However, after a few days we knew we didn't want to cry anymore, even though we easily could have, we wanted to stay positive and strong for Ava. We told our family to try and do the same and only ever be positive around her when visiting. It felt important now more than ever to stop being my normal pessimistic self. That may have been okay when it was about my own personal issues, but I knew Ava deserved better. She needed hope, so I dove into the depths of my mind, my body, and my soul, and I told myself that this time I would do it differently, for her.

Ava had weekly scans and the week after the news, the bleed was continuing but we had no further new information. The doctors said they were shocked because other than a little bit of apnoea, she didn't present as a baby with a bleed, and had they not scanned her they wouldn't have known for some time. At her two week scan they told us that the bleed had stopped, but in doing so it had clotted and was blocking the flow of cerebral spinal fluid which was causing a build-up of pressure in Ava's head. They planned to watch this closely and measure her head constantly, as she may end up needing an operation.

When Ava was three weeks old I had my psychology appointment. It meant that I could only fit in a short visit with Ava that day. Lisa took me, which I appreciated because it meant I wasn't alone and in my head on the way there, and I could chat to her on the way home. We arrived in plenty of time for my appointment, I walked in and only had a short wait before I seeing the psychologist, Sarah. She asked how I was, and I began to tell her what had happened the past few weeks. The second she heard that I'd had the baby she said, "Sorry, can I stop you there. I can't do the assessment, I'm so sorry". My initial thought was that she felt I should be at the hospital with Ava and not there with her and that it was inappropriate for Social Services to ask me to go at that time. I begged her to continue, explaining that this had been a huge stress on me for weeks, and it would be a blessing to have it behind me because I knew that mentally I was doing well. Sarah told me that, unfortunately, she was unable to do the assessment because if it went to court, the assessment would be void for having been conducted in the first eight weeks after birth. Owing to all the hormones in my system, you're not supposed to carry out a psychological assessment on anyone until eight weeks post-partum. She explained that she had emailed Social Services to tell them and asked to be informed if I had the baby, and they replied saying they would, yet they hadn't. I should not have been sent there.

To say I was upset was an understatement. I wanted to be with my critically ill daughter and Social Services had me hours away for nothing. I couldn't help but cry from frustration. Sarah and I both called around Social Services to ask what they wanted us to do. She said she was willing to go ahead if they wanted her to, but they needed to be made aware that it wouldn't be a valid assessment if it went to court. When she told them this, they told her not to do it, and that we would re-book.

Sarah and I sat and spoke, and I asked that when they re-book, it would be helpful if she could possibly do the two sessions in one extended visit. I explained that I would rather do that because, knowing it couldn't happen for another five weeks at the very least, this would take us close to when the doctors may allow Ava to come home. If the report wasn't completed it was highly likely that Social Services wouldn't let us take Ava home at all and she would be placed into foster care. Sarah said she would try and help, adding that in her opinion she had seen enough in the last fifteen minutes to know that mentally, I was doing well, coping with this situation given everything I had going on at home. Sarah was angry with the actions of Social Services and I found comfort in having my feelings validated.

With the assessment cancelled, I went to straight to see Ava. At the hospital, I was told that they were concerned about the pressure building up in Ava's head, and that she was close to needing an operation, but needed to be transferred to Leeds General Infirmary as they didn't do that kind of operation there. I phoned Stewart and he prepared a bag for me and Ava, and I went in the ambulance with my little girl, while Stewart stayed at home. I couldn't let her go alone and I knew Stewart needed to work because he had no paid leave left, and without his work we would struggle financially with our rent and bills. Knowing we had harder days ahead, we had to strategically choose when he took unpaid leave, to minimise the pressure this placed on our finances.

Pulling into Leeds just after midnight, I'd never been to this hospital and it was huge. Compared to our small local hospital it was very intimidating and I knew I'd end up getting lost walking those corridors. Ava was put on the newborns surgical ward, which was one big room with cartoon walls with bright colours. There's a nurse's desk in the centre of the room and the babies have their cots or incubators along the edges of the room. I stayed with Ava until they had connected her to the machines, and I knew what would be happening. There was some discussion about whether Ava's case was so urgent that she needed emergency surgery, but after looking at her they decided to wait until the morning.

I could have stayed in the hospital in a room right next to the ward that night, but I could hear every cry and bleep from every machine from Ava's ward, and the staff running in and out constantly. I tried to sleep, and I tried to stay in the room, but I couldn't. I was having constant panic attacks, rushing and intrusive thoughts, and I was unable to stop crying. I needed to stay close by, but I couldn't stay in the hospital. I needed my own space and some comfort because I felt close to breaking down, and Ava needed her mum to be her best self. At 3am, I walked into the lobby of a hotel in Leeds city centre. I had called ahead to explain the situation and the concierge was so kind he booked me into a deluxe room, for a standard room price. As soon as my head hit the pillow, I was asleep.

My alarm was set for 6am and I met Stewart at 8am. He took the day off work and would stay with me for the weekend. We headed to the hospital and waited for news on Ava's brain surgery, which was expected to be in the morning but by lunch time, she had been bumped to a few hours later by several emergencies. It was clear that Ava was now in significant pain because she was crying a lot and being sick quite often, even though she hadn't been given a feed yet that day because of her op being scheduled. They had decided to fit what they called an access device into Ava's head. They could then put a needle into this device and drain the fluid manually. They were hoping this pressure would be temporary and therefore they would only need to do this a few times, after which it would be done on an 'as needed' basis.

The time came for Ava to go for surgery. We chose to wave her off from the ward instead of watching as they put her to sleep, as I knew that would be much more distressing than I could handle. We made sure that Ralph the elephant went with her, as he'd gone with her to all her scans, and we didn't want her to be without something familiar. As they wheeled her away, I broke down in tears and we walked out of the hospital, I hadn't eaten for well over 24 hours and, although food was the last thing on my mind, I knew I needed to eat.

We rushed through lunch, eager to get back to the hospital, even though I knew they would call when the surgery was done. We sat in a café on the bottom floor of the children's wing and talked about insignificant things. Each second of every minute seemed to be longer than the last. The worry running through my mind was immense. Every time I heard anything that vaguely sounded like the phone ringing, I would jump. Looking around, I recognised that other people in the café likely had their own struggles. We usually walk past people and we don't notice that they exist, we don't think why they're in the hospital. Maybe they're visiting poorly family, or they work here, and saved a life today, or not and it was a bad shift for them. You can't go through this kind of thing without suddenly coming to the realisation that everyone could be suffering. I'm an empathic person, and this realisation, of the potential suffering of others, amplified my own.

After almost three hours, our phone finally rang to say our little girl was through her surgery and was being taken back to the ward, we could come and see her once she was there. As soon as I hung up the phone, Stewart started to cry. He'd been holding in his pain all this time, quietly scared of something going wrong. He doesn't wear his heart on his sleeve the way I do, and it hurt to know he had been hiding his feelings, and I reassured him he didn't need to with me. We were equal, we were in this together, and we both deserved to show our feelings, and to feel supported by each other. We cried together for a few minutes before heading for the ward.

Ava was more awake than I had expected, but this was short lived, and she soon looked exhausted. She was a little pale and worse for wear, but what three-week-old wouldn't be after three hours of brain surgery? We stayed and talked to her and stared at her as if we were seeing her again for the very first time. It was painful beyond belief to know Ava was suffering, but I knew the doctors were doing their best to save her life. After being told she would need a lot of rest over the next few days, and to protect her from infections, we cut our visits short. We all needed our strength to survive this.

Chapter Thirty-Three
Her Fight - Part Two

Ava was doing well and got through the first 48 hours after her surgery with no signs of infection. The doctor came on the first day and drained and measured fluid from the access device that had been fitted in her head. This would need doing every few days and the volume that drained, along with measurements of Ava's head, would tell them if the access device worked, or whether they needed to do something else. Unfortunately, over the next few days, they needed to manually drain more fluid than they were comfortable with, and it became obvious the device wasn't working. Ava was showing signs of being in pain and distress again, her heart rate was all over the place, her oxygen levels kept dropping and she also started to cry a lot more. Exactly a week after her first brain surgery, she was taken in for a second.

For this surgery, they were fitting a shunt into the back of her head. This had a wire that travelled through her body into her abdomen, so the fluid from her head could be released automatically into her abdomen and then absorbed into her body. It was a slightly longer surgery, with the possibility of needing to go into intensive care afterwards. Hearing the words 'intensive care', scared me so much. Even though I knew all of this was dangerous and a risk to her life, hearing the doctors saying 'intensive care' felt like they were warning there was an even greater chance that she may not survive.

Ava went down into surgery at roughly the same time as she had done the week before. Yet again, we said goodbye to our daughter, just in case the worst happened.

Ralph kept her company once more and Stewart and I walked through the hospital, with me sobbing. Back we went to the Wetherspoons across from the hospital where I once again forced myself to have something to eat despite feeling sick with worry. It was a replay of the previous experience with me checking my phone repeatedly, while all around me people went about their business. I wondered if their day was as tense as mine. I saw other customers chatting and laughing. I noticed the hard-working staff member who seemed rushed off his feet and, as he cleared a table a plate of leftover food fell to the floor and made a mess. How I'd give anything for something so seemingly simple to be the worst part of my day.

Just like the previous surgery, I silently acknowledged that I know nothing about the lives of those around me, their troubles and worries are a mystery. Just as they have no idea, they are sat next to two petrified parents; the only indication was the mother quietly wiping away tears. They don't know that this mother is, once again, waiting for the most important phone call of her life. A call to tell her that her daughter is still alive. Or not. I imagined the dreaded phone call a thousand different ways. The good, the bad and even the earth shattering. Until I picked up the phone, I wouldn't know which call I'd get.

Walking back to the hospital, I mentioned that it had been two hours and I was getting nervous. Stewart assured me that everything would be fine and that we would hear from the surgery team soon. That word 'soon'. I hated that word. I feel like it's said to people in situations when they are eagerly awaiting something specific, in which case 'soon' is never soon enough. We sat in the waiting area of the entrance to the children's wing of the hospital. Déjà vu following us around. After what seemed like an eternity, and after letting myself release some fear and having a good cry, the phone rang. It was a withheld number, and I gave a stern word to myself not to yell if it was a telemarketing call. It wasn't. Ava was out of surgery and would be back in the newborns surgical ward shortly as she didn't need to stay in the ICU. All had gone well. The weight of the world was lifted once more.

This thing happens when you have a baby, or at least it had for me, possibly due to the more complex situation surrounding Ava. It was a need, a want, a deep and meaningful urge to see my baby every second of the day. I looked at Ava and I took in every little thing about her. Every hair, every small raise of her chest as she breathed, every feature. I knew that just a few weeks ago, I functioned perfectly well having never met this tiny human, but now I needed to see her as much as possible. I wanted to know everything about her. Obviously, if we were your average family, Ava would be at home and we would be with her all the time but some families, like ours, have to go through a period where they must trust others to do their job. When I was at the unit in the hospital, and heard other babies cry and the nurses couldn't tend to them straight away, it pained me because I know that when Ava cried and I wasn't there, she likely wasn't comforted immediately either. I know some parents have a different parenting style and they choose not to run to their child at every murmur, but I admit that I am that 'run to their child' kind of parent. I felt like Ava's cry was directly tuned in to my heart and it broke at the first sound of upset from her, so I instinctively needed to comfort her. After the difficulties we'd suffered with parenthood thus far, I was definitely that kind of parent. So, in the time that I was with Ava at the hospital, I could do nothing but fall ever more in love with her as I soaked in her every detail. I saw her smile (yes, I know it wasn't a 'real' smile, but I would take what I could get) and something inside me felt more content than I had been in a very long time. Being with Ava, watching every twitch, grin and movement and hearing every little noise, gurgle, and breath, I knew that there would never be a day again where I didn't want to see Ava. I was utterly infatuated with her. A mother, totally in love.

When we got to the ward, a familiar site greeted us as she laid with her eyes beaming. She looked so battered and bruised and a section of her hair was now gone from the back of her head, and you could see the shunt underneath creating a visible lump. The doctors said it was swelling and, although it would go down, we would always be able to feel it; although when her hair grew out we wouldn't be able to see it.

For the next 24 hours, Ava's oxygen levels and heartrate didn't improve, and Ava was given a blood transfusion. When we visited her the next morning, she already looked so much better and seemed livelier. I had always called Ava a wriggler, she was so active in the womb and even in her incubator they had to make sure she had something around her to limit her moving. Babies are positioned face down, so they don't get sore being in one spot for too long, but Ava didn't like it and used her strong legs to push off her incubator bed.

It was hard to believe that while this was going on, I had social services phoning the hospital for updates on Ava. At such a critical time, they couldn't focus on correcting their mistakes and arranging another assessment, instead they felt it acceptable to be inserting themselves into Ava's care while she was in hospital, like they hadn't dropped the ball with their handling of our case. It angered me that they couldn't take a step back and use the time to sort things out behind the scenes. It seemed unnecessary to be calling asking the nursing staff for updates about when Ava could come home, when she was fighting for her life.

After a few days, Ava was improving fast. She had stopped being sick, her heartrate was normal and her oxygen levels, though still dropping randomly and briefly, were good enough for us to return to our local hospital. It took a few days to arrange because the ambulance transportation was run by a charity staffed by volunteer paramedics. We returned to our hospital exactly two weeks after we had left, and we were so relieved to be back. All Ava had to do now was remain stable and grow, and eventually she would come home; Social Services permitting.

Chapter Thirty-Four
Home

Three weeks later, Ava was doing so well that she had graduated into the last room in the ward and was now out of an incubator and into an open cot. For parents on the NICU ward, these are big milestones, and I was overjoyed to walk in and see her in an open cot for the first time. The next move after that is going home, if Social Services allow us! We had been discussing dates for a while, now Ava had begun to feed with a bottle without being as sick. Her head was growing but at a normal rate and she was steadily gaining weight. She was still laying on an apnoea mat, as she would sometimes forget to breathe, but this was becoming less frequent, and we could take the mat home with us, although the idea of that filled me with fear.

At the end of August, we planned for CJ and RJ to come with Peggy to the hospital to meet Ava. The ward only allowed children to visit if they were siblings. As the nurses were aware that Social Services were involved, I had to give a brief explanation of who the boys were ahead of their visit, so they weren't mistakenly turned away when they arrived. The boys felt special being allowed to come and see her and it would have been horrible it they had been refused entry after a two-hour drive.

The nurses we'd grown close to were excited to see the boys meet Ava, and every time the buzzer went they got excited in case it was them. When they finally arrived, all the nurses bobbed their heads out of rooms to catch a look at the boys, and took brisk walks past our room to create the opportunity of glancing in. Later, a few told me they had teared up; that our story of reunion and contact had moved them. It was a great day for everyone, though there wasn't much for the boys to do they seemed to want to spend a lot of time with Ava, and we made sure to get a photo of us all together. It was surreal to think that CJ and RJ were both back in the hospital they were born in, over a decade later and after being adopted, yet here they were, with me, watching over their little sister. Despite being taken from my care, they were still part of the big moments, which meant a lot to me and I hope it will mean a lot to them as they grow up. Peggy and Chris have certainly given so much back to us since our contact began.

There was a suggestion that we could bring Ava home on her original due date, and it was glaringly obvious that time was becoming an issue for getting the psychology assessment done. Sarah needed to do the assessment, write the report and send it to the Social Services Panel, who then needed time to read it and make their decision.

The day of my assessment came. This time Lisa couldn't take me, but Social Services agreed to book a taxi and, luckily, the driver was chatty, so the journey was pleasant and mostly kept my mind busy. On arrival, I completed a few questionnaires while waiting, that provided a basic score on how I was currently doing, regarding certain mental health issues such as anxiety and depression. I made sure to note on them that I would appreciate it if my current circumstances, with Ava being in hospital and Social Services being slow with their decision, could be taken into consideration when calculating any score. It wasn't enough that a piece of paper says I am anxious or feeling low, without looking at why, and Social Services and their delays and stress were a big part of my current worries. There's a big difference between someone who is uncontrollably in a mental downward spiral, and someone who is aware of why they are feeling the way they are and is managing their feelings appropriately.

I was adamant that any mental health issues I may currently be experiencing should not be used as a reason to stop Ava from coming home.

If Social Services did stop us bringing Ava home, then our Plan B was that I would find somewhere else to stay, in the interim, while Social Services completed their assessment. It would not be an ideal situation, denying us the right to family life, but we believed it was more important for Ava to come home than it was for me to be there when she did. During the last few weeks of the pregnancy, I had met up with Peggy who had generously paid for me to engage a solicitor. Since Social Services seemed to be dragging their feet getting an assessment sorted, we wanted to know if there was anything the solicitor could do to put pressure on them to make things move faster. Unfortunately, there wasn't, but we felt it was good that Social Services knew I had someone representing me. I wasn't the quiet, naïve, vulnerable young girl I was the first time I went through this.

After about 45 minutes in the waiting room, Sarah called me in to start the assessment. Most of this was just the two of us talking. I caught her up on what happened after I left her office last time and everything that had happened since. We discussed how I was currently feeling and who I had for support. Then she started to ask me questions regarding the old report and we talked about it in detail. I was fully open and honest about every aspect of it all. When I was younger and I was talking to the psychologist who wrote the first report, I was so scared that a lot of what I said was either what I thought she wanted to hear, or something that Jason had told me to say to gain sympathy. I knew the results of that initial assessment had been clouded by my inability to be honest, I didn't want that to happen again, and after my therapy, I was no longer afraid of telling the truth. The assessment ended after a few hours and I felt confident. Even though Sarah couldn't tell me directly what she thought, she very sincerely said that I had nothing to worry about, and I knew in that moment that there wasn't going to be anything Social Services could do to stop Ava from coming home.

The assessment took place on Thursday, the 5th of September 2019. Ava was due to be discharged on her original due date of the 15th of September; six working days after the assessment. To make matters worse, the 15th was a Sunday, which meant we needed an answer by the Friday. I know people may wonder why we didn't just move the date of her coming home. After waiting for so long to have Ava, and for her to be healthy enough to come home, the idea of changing that date simply to suit Social Services, fell way short of being okay with me. There was a principle involved; if Ava could come home, then she should come home. Being home with her parents is what was best for her, it was where she belonged. Keeping her in hospital because Social Services had been inefficient was morally wrong.

We heard on Tuesday the 10th of September that the report was in and I knew they wouldn't read it in time. We asked someone to skim read it because, after reading it myself it was clear that Sarah had no concerns whatsoever about my mental health, or my ability to be a good parent. She even wrote that there was no evidence of the mental health issues mentioned in the first report. When I read that, I thought surely they would allow Ava to come home. We knew they would still need to be involved in some capacity, but the report supported my Social Worker's recommendation that they didn't need to take my parental rights from me.

We learnt on the Thursday, through my solicitor, that because Social Services hadn't taken us to court to take over parental rights, we could take Ava home whether they said so or not. We had every right to do so, and it would have been up to them to stop us by getting an emergency injunction, however, that's not how I wanted to take my daughter home. I wanted it to be with their say so. I wanted to do this right and not muddy the waters. I didn't need to resort to tactics like these though; I knew they had no reason to say we couldn't take Ava home with us. I wasn't the scared, vulnerable teenager with no experience of care proceedings that I was once upon a time with CJ's case. I was 31-year-old with knowledge of the way the system worked, and the confidence to speak up for myself and to advocate for my child. I was done with life knocking me down and expecting me to stay there. I had a daughter who needed me to be better than that. I couldn't be strong enough for CJ and RJ, I couldn't be strong enough for myself so many times; but I could be strong for Ava now.

On the Friday, deadline day, one of the nurses who had gotten to know us and our story, repeatedly rang Social Services all morning for us. I felt confident and my Mama Bear had been activated. I was calling Social Services myself and asking my solicitor to do the same. It was quite literally taking a team of people to get a quick response from them. Nothing was happening, it seemed like getting a simple 'yes, they can take her home', was impossible for them. I didn't know what else they needed. We were told they would call the nurses station as soon as they got the word. Each time the phone rang, I jumped up thinking this was the time. It rang many times but was never the call we were waiting for. Until it was. The nurse came running in saying we had the green light. At the same time, I got a message from Kate saying we could take Ava home, she had come in on her day off and got the job done for us. She was my hero! I cried with relief knowing that within 48 hours, our baby would be home.

On the Sunday, we arrived with Ava's car seat, ready to take her home and I was giddy like a kid at Christmas as I dressed Ava in her going home outfit. The one her Daddy had originally picked was still far too big for her, so we chose one that was sent to us by a friend from across the pond in the USA. It was a blue sleepsuit with little white elephants on it, and it had a matching hat too. I had been packing up Ava's things throughout the morning, so this was already done. I was very eager to finally get out of that hospital. We strapped Ava into her car seat, put Ralph across her lap, said goodbye to the nurses, and took our baby home.

Chapter Thirty-Five

Scars

The first few weeks with Ava were bliss. Our Social Worker, Kate, visited every few days and I also met my health visitor, and an outreach worker who came to measure Ava's head to check it wasn't growing quicker than it should, and to help with any questions we had about Ava's shunt. There was regular communication between us all to keep Social Services updated on how Ava was doing, and how I was doing too.

Although Ava was allowed home with us, we later learned there was a clause attached that I couldn't be left alone with Ava until the Panel had read the full report and come to a formal decision. This meant Stewart had to take an unpaid week off work, because he had passed the threshold to book any paternity leave off. That this clause put us under great financial strain seemed to be of no concern to Social Services. We had no choice but to, once again, meet their demands. At every stage of the process, Social Services expected things that caused us a great deal of stress, during one of the most trying times we'd ever faced. We were bending over backwards to accommodate their short comings, something that didn't appear to be recognised or appreciated. We were not the problem; the problem was Social Services' processes, which were a classic case of the tail wagging the dog.

A week later, the Panel had read the report and placed Ava under a Child in Need order. This meant we would receive regular visits for the next six months and, if everything was okay after that time, Social Services would sign us off. I was happy to do this because I had grown anxious about whether I was doing everything right and knowing I had extra support here and there helped. Now the involvement of Social Services was focused on helping me to do my best instead of dragging me down.

Initially, Kate visited weekly by herself, and monthly with all of us present: the health visitor, outreach worker, myself, and Kate. For the first meeting with everyone, I asked Lisa to join us. From experience, I had never been in a meeting with people like that and come out of it positively. It had always been bad. Because of the history of having Social Services judge me, I had been left terrified of doing anything wrong, and assumed that I was doing nothing right. I had no confidence. I wanted Ava home, but once she was, I so scared of anything going wrong in case they took her away too, that I was living in fear of being her mum. Having Lisa there for moral support meant a lot to me. The meeting went very well, and everyone was encouraging and kind; they kept saying I was doing a fantastic job, and I ended up crying because I wasn't used to praise when it came to motherhood. I had such a hard time believing them when they said I was doing well, that it was overwhelming. Having my motherhood taken from me had left a lot of scars that I didn't know were there until I became Mum again.

I found my motherly instinct in fighting for Social Services to get done what they needed to do to get our daughter home. But once home, their looming presence in my past life left a stain on my day-to-day parenting. I questioned everything I did; I didn't feel comfortable leaving Ava with anyone other than her Dad. I'd sit with Ava, by her side constantly. I know part of this was due to her medical conditions, but I couldn't help but think that I'd do that even if she didn't have medical issues. I had this constant feeling that I had to be with her at every moment. That was the only way I knew to keep her safe. I hoped that time would heal these wounds, as Ava grew, and I became more confident.

Before Christmas, Peggy and I messaged each other, and I brought up wanting to re-start the podcast. Though I hadn't expected returning to it so soon, I wanted something to lift my spirits and something to focus on, as well as being Mum. It was a way of bringing balance into my life. Peggy was more than happy to start again, and she purchased the equipment while I started designing our Two Good Mums logo. We started planning the episodes in more detail and arranged to start recording in January.

Ava was growing well and though she showed some delays, these were not unexpected. We were still very happy to watch her learn to smile and become more aware of the world around her. We celebrated her first Christmas with our family, and it was everything we had ever dreamt of. I have never spent Christmas Day with my child before. I strived to make it perfect, even though Ava had no idea what was going on. We left out cookies and milk for Santa and a carrot for Rudolph. I made sure the decorations were perfect and we got Ava a matching stocking for our mantle, one that exactly matched the ones we'd bought almost seven years earlier. I had unsuccessfully scoured the internet for years looking for that beautiful stocking, hoping that one day we would get to use it. I'm glad I never gave up hoping, because, when Ava came home and Christmas approached, I looked one more time and this time it was there!

We bought Ava a Christmas Eve pyjama set, just as we do for ourselves each year. Ava's had 'My First Christmas' written on it. For Christmas day, we chose a plaid dress with ivory tights and the cutest Christmas pudding shoes for her to wear to Stewart's mums. Then to go to my Mum's, we changed her into a deep red dress with shimmering glitter and white tights with ruby baby shoes. For Christmas night, she wore a red first Christmas sleepsuit. It was the perfect first Christmas as a family of three.

After Christmas and New Year, Kate said she would start visiting monthly as Social Services recognised how well I had been doing with Ava. I knew we didn't have long to go until we would be signed off. Yet even though this momentous event was just around the corner, I still couldn't let myself fully believe it would happen. I kept thinking that, at any moment, someone would see that I was a horrible mum, and it would all be taken away again. However, the more time that passed without this happening, the more I started to believe in myself.

January arrived and it was time for Peggy and me to finally start recording the podcast we'd been speaking about for over a year and a half. We met at the university Peggy was attending, and where she booked a quiet room to record on Saturdays. In each episode, we told a part of our adoption journey, from beginning to where we were now. In February, Peggy was invited to speak at a One Adoption conference, and I was invited along too. Even though we hadn't finished recording all the episodes, we used that occasion to announce our podcast to everyone. Peggy's presentation was a brief account of our adoption journey and the benefits of direct contact, and what was needed for it to work. She used our story as a positive example and introduced me, and I joined the Q&A panel at the end of the day.

The conference was the first time I had ever been in a room with another birth mum, Clarissa, something that didn't dawn on me until later in the day. Clarissa also made a presentation that day and she is the co-founder of Re-Frame, an organisation specialising in supporting birth mums, and is a well-known advocate in the sector. I was so thankful to meet her and was in awe of her strength to stand up and tell her story to a room full of professionals, unafraid, at least on the surface, of judgement. I've looked up to Clarissa ever since that day. I realised something even more profound that day. It was the first time I had ever been publicly acknowledged as the boys' birth mum. While we don't show photos of the boys anywhere online, the people at this conference were privy to photos from our meet ups. Nobody outside of our circle, or who wasn't a professional linked to our case, had ever seen a photo of me with the boys after they were removed from my care. I hadn't been connected to them like this since their births.

The fact that we only ever got praised for the way we handled our contact and our situation, made me realise I shouldn't be afraid of the title of Mum. Not in relation to the boys. It was something I had spent so much time running away from, I felt so undeserving of it after Social Services had torn my confidence down with their damning judgement of me, that I couldn't bear to be called it anymore. I didn't feel like I had been a mum to them because I didn't do any of the things a normal mum did, like teach them to tie their shoes, tuck them in at night, or help them with homework. After seeing Peggy's presentation and seeing the impact it had on the people in the room, I realised I had been a mum in the best way I could, with the situation I was faced with. I always put the boys' needs first and that's what a mum does. After that, I was proud to be their birth mum.

We received great feedback from the conference and started gaining a small social media following, which spurred us on to finish the podcast faster than we had originally planned. Our launch date, for the release of the first podcast episode, was April 10th, Good Friday. Our social media pages were all up and running and we had people interacting with us who had seen us at the conference and were excited to hear the podcast.

Kate visited at the end of February and, although she didn't think she needed to come again, it was not her decision. Given that the Panel had never previously followed her recommendations, I didn't put much weight on what she said, and assumed I'd be seeing her at least one more time. I kept telling myself that they may even extend it; still feeling I wasn't good enough. On March 9th, I got a text from Kate; short and sweet. 'Hi Laura, you're signed off, I'll send you the minutes by post when I get a minute'. I had to read the text several times before it sunk in. I messaged Stewart with the news, I rang Mum who cried down the phone, and I messaged Lisa too and then I posted on Facebook. I wanted to go to the highest mountain and scream it at the top of my lungs. This journey to parenthood has been long, gruelling, heart-breaking, life altering and so incredibly hard that it has changed me for life. For me, this journey started in 2005 when I was pregnant with CJ. The day that I was told Ava was ours to keep and Social Services would no longer be involved, was the day it ended, and it was one of the best days of my entire life. I had waited 14 long years for those words, 'you're signed off'. It was strange that after everything they had put us through, the end came through a simple text. We jumped through every one of their hoops, we had endured emotional, psychological, and financial pressure, yet we weren't worthy of the time to send an official final response in writing. As I write this in April 2021, over a year after being ever so casually 'signed off', I am still waiting to receive official written confirmation.

It's not easy to be a mum again after the shame of having a child removed. Throughout Ava's first year, I doubted myself more times than I ever had before. I'd felt like a fraud, someone pretending and waiting to be found out. Some days were hard, and I'd questioned whether Social Services should have taken Ava; not for any reason other than I felt that I wasn't good enough. Ava has had difficulties over the months as she's grown but, luckily, her shunt hasn't yet caused any issues. She is thriving as best she can, and she is the happiest baby I have ever known. But the scars left from Social Services are burnt deep into my psyche. After what I've been through, I don't think it is going to be possible to ever be a normal parent. I will always worry when Ava trips and scrapes her knee, I will always blame myself and question my abilities when she gets an innocent bump from learning to crawl or walk. I am learning to try and protect Ava, while maintaining a distance that allows her to explore her capabilities as a toddler and discover the world around her. It's a learning curve for both of us.

The scars of my experiences with Social Services are healing, but they still itch. I wonder if I will ever feel that I have the right to be a mum, or whether I will always feel like a fraud. I know it will take a lot of work, but I hope I get there before Ava's childhood is gone. I fought so hard to get here, and yet I may still miss it all if I'm trapped in a cycle of self-doubt and fear that history will repeat itself and I am destined to forever feel loss.

In the run up to Ava's first birthday I had been incredibly emotional. Eventually I made a vague connection that it was something to do with Ava, the child I got to keep. Still, I couldn't understand why I felt so low, on edge and upset. Then I had an epiphany; I was feeling so horrible because of my experience of the boys' first birthdays. Ava's first birthday was triggering the demon ghosts of birthdays past.

I'd been dreaming of making Ava's first birthday as perfect as possible. I hadn't done this before outside of a Social Services office, without being watched and judged. Sometimes I still feel eyes on me and hold my breath in anticipation of being told I'm not doing things right. I've come to realise the only person watching and judging me now, is me!

During the period leading up to Ava's birthday I ugly cried multiple times a day because I've never had the opportunity to celebrate a first birthday properly before. And when I cried, someone always reminded me that I am a good mum. Yet the deep-rooted trauma from my experiences with Social Services manifested as a cloud of anxiety surrounding Ava turning one. Both the boys' first birthdays came with the knowledge that I didn't have much time left with them. And now, even though Social Services are no longer involved in our lives, my traumatised brain was preparing to lose Ava.

I wanted Ava's first birthday to be the best I could make it, and nothing less would do. Despite a global pandemic, I was determined to make it special for her yet, at the same time, I was putting a relentless pressure on myself. But I painted on a smile and held my daughter for dear life as she turned one, while my heart throbbed with expectations of future misery; born from the trauma of forced adoption.

Epilogue
Final Thoughts

The aftereffects of losing children to forced adoption has left me with scars that may well be with me forever. But I strongly believe that I have ended up where I was always meant to be. I often now say that I no longer regret what happened, with the boys being adopted, I only regret how it happened; that CJ was injured. I will carry that with me for the rest of my life.

Now I have my husband and my beautiful daughter, Ava, it's too hard to say that I wish things had been different. Being led down this path, with the boys being adopted, has given rise to some pretty amazing things. CJ and RJ have a happy and fulfilled life with their parents, two of the most remarkable people I have ever met. Out of the ashes of heartbreak, we have forged a new kind of family, one I could have never imagined, but will be forever thankful for.

For me and Stewart, Ava will be our only child. We will spend the rest of our lives together loving on our little miracle and enjoying life as the family that we fought so very hard to create. There's no way to come out of a journey like mine unscathed, but when Ava was born my ability to hope was reborn with her. I have faith that she can show me how to live life to the full and she can teach me how to love without fear. I can hold her forevermore, knowing she gets to stay with us. Never to part. Baby of Mine.

Printed in Great Britain
by Amazon

86597129R00123